MEN-AT-ARMS SERIES

EDITOR: MARTIN WINDROW
with
DENNIS BALDRY

Battle for the Falklands (3) Air Forces

Text by ROY BRAYBROOK

Colour plates by MICHAEL ROFFE,
TERRY HADLER and MICHAEL CHAPPELL

OSPREY PUBLISHING LONDON

First published November 1982
Reprinted November 1982, March 1983, May 1984

34144

Published in 1982 by
Osprey Publishing Ltd
Member company of the George Philip Group
12–14 Long Acre, London WC2E 9LP
© Copyright 1982 Osprey Publishing Ltd
Reprinted 1986, 1987, 1988

British Library Cataloguing in Publication Data

Battle for the Falklands.—(Men-at-Arms series; 135)
  3: Air forces
  1. Falkland Islands War, 1982
  I. Braybrook, Roy   II. Series
  997.11   F3031

  ISBN 0-85045-493-X

Filmset in England by
Tameside Filmsetting Limited
Ashton-under-Lyne, Lancashire

Printed in Hong Kong

Editor's Note:
The publishers are grateful for the generous assistance
of the following during the preparation of this book:
George Balin, John Chappell, Geoff Cornish, Adrian
English, Simon Dunstan, Stuart Finn, Bruce Kamiat,
Lee Russell, Steve Zaloga; and the Still Photo
Branch, Office of Information, Dept. of the Navy,
Washington DC. They also feel that under the
circumstances it may be desirable to note that a
donation has been made to the South Atlantic Fund.

Battle for the Falklands (3) Air Forces

Introduction

In assessing the contribution made by air power to the Falklands conflict, it must first be stated that the islands were taken by Argentina on 2 April and retaken by Britain on 14 June by soldiers and marines, the majority of whom had landed from ships; hence it may be argued that ground and naval forces played the key roles.

However, aircraft (both fixed and rotary-wing) were of crucial importance to both sides: in moving reinforcements quickly across the sea and over the islands, in attacking surface vessels, and in providing protection (with varying degrees of success) against attacks from both above and below the waves. The role of air power was thus to assist friendly surface forces in the execution of their duties, while hindering enemy forces in theirs.

The air arms of the two antagonists consequently functioned in what was essentially a supporting

Heavy weather in the TEZ: in Force 10 gales the Sea Harriers are securely lashed down to the deck of HMS *Hermes.* **'18' has an AIM-9L Sidewinder visible on the outboard starboard pylon. (MoD)**

Two Sea Harriers, both fuelled and one armed, on the crowded flight deck of HMS *Hermes* early in the carrier group's voyage south; although these two are already displaying 'warpaint', another in the background is still in its two-tone peacetime scheme. (MoD)

role, but an important one, nonetheless. The British Task Force might have sailed without any other ship, but its commander, Adm. Woodward, is reliably reported to have said that it could not have sailed without HMS *Hermes*, the larger of the two aircraft carriers.

On the Argentine side, it is extremely unlikely that a major operation would have been mounted against the Falklands if the islands had been beyond the reach of land-based combat aircraft. As we shall see later, the distances involved for both sides made it a marginal operation for most of the aircraft involved; yet air power was an essential ingredient in the overall force-mix.

Furthermore, the air war in the South Atlantic was of historical importance for at least three reasons. Firstly, the distances from the bases to the combat zone broke several records for long-range, long-endurance operations. Secondly, air-launched, sea-skimming, anti-ship stand-off missiles (the British Aerospace Sea Skua and the

Aérospatiale AM.39 Exocet) were to be used in earnest for the first time. Thirdly, the Falklands conflict was the first occasion that high-performance V/STOL combat aircraft were tested under real war conditions.

Derived from the Hawker P.1127 (first flown in 1960), the Harrier had just missed seeing action with the US Marine Corps as the AV-8A in the Vietnam War. It had been operated by the RAF from dispersed sites in Germany during war games, and it had been flown successfully in mock combat against conventional fighters; but this radical new concept had never experienced the ultimate test of a shooting war.

The main questions were, whether the Harrier's much-publicised ability to operate from a wide variety of small ships and from small dispersed sites on land would prove of real value; and whether its effectiveness in low/medium-level combat against conventional supersonic fighters would live up to the advertising. The conflict in the South Atlantic could thus well decide the future for V/STOL combat aircraft development, the only form of military aviation in which Britain can justly claim a world lead.

4

The Problems

At the outset, the tasks facing the Argentine air arms were rapidly to reinforce their island garrison; to prevent British shipping approaching the Falklands; to base close support aircraft and helicopters on the islands to oppose possible landings; and to safeguard Argentine cities, ports, and military installations against air attack. For Britain, the corresponding tasks were to establish an air bridge between the UK and the staging post of Wideawake airbase on Ascension Island (and later, on a smaller scale, from Wideawake to the Task Force); to safeguard Ascension against a possible Entebbe-style attack; to provide ASW (anti-submarine warfare) cover, and later air defence, for the Task Force against attacks expected both from Argentine land bases and from the carrier *Veinticinco de Mayo*; to support amphibious landings and subsequent ground action on the Falklands; and also to maintain a credible threat of strikes against Argentina, to pin down at least part of their Mirage interceptor force in domestic air defence duties.

Argentina had spent freely in the late 1970s to expand her armed forces in the expectation of a war with Chile over control of the Beagle Channel. That dispute had been patched over, leaving the Argentine Air Force (Fuerza Aerea Argentina: FAA) one of the strongest in Latin America, well equipped with combat aircraft, and with vast stocks of bombs, rockets, and ammunition. Due to internal security problems, the FAA was also strong in COIN (counter-insurgency) aircraft, with approximately 60 IA.58 Pucará ground-attack aircraft delivered out of the 100 on order. However, the service was not a well-balanced force in terms of equipment, having only seven C-130E/H Hercules transport aircraft, and two KC-130H tankers.

The standard reference sources describe the FAA's fighter element as consisting of approximately 19 Dassault-Breguet Mirage IIIEA's, two IIIDA two-seaters, and 26 similar but Israeli-built Daggers—Mirage 5s. A further batch of 14 is now believed to have been supplied by Israel. All these aircraft were also capable of ground attack or anti-shipping missions, which were the roles of the service's 60–odd Douglas A-4P Skyhawks, aircraft that had served previously with the US Navy as A-4B/Cs. (The first 50 were converted A-4Bs, the remainder A-4Cs.) Although long in the tooth, these Skyhawks could still provide a useful warload-radius performance, and in the last 25 aircraft the original simple reflector gunsights had been replaced by Ferranti ISIS D–126R predictor sights for better weapon delivery accuracy. For long-range strikes with heavier loads, the service still operated six Canberra B.62s, backed by a pair of T.64 operational trainers.

From the British viewpoint, the Argentine air force alone might thus be expected to field roughly 120–180 combat aircraft, depending on whether or not the turboprop Pucarás were included. It is of interest to note that the service's commander, Brig.Gen. Basilio Lami Dozo, has been reported as stating that he began the conflict with 84 combat

ARGENTINE AIRBASES

A: Buenos Aires/El Palomar
B: Moron
C: Tandil
D: Rosario
E: Santa Fe/Reconquista
F: Parana/Gen. Urquiza
G: Oran
H: Jujuy
I: Salta
J: San Miguel de Tucuman
K: Resistancia
L: San Juan
M: El Plumerillo
N: Cordoba
O: Villa Mercedes
P: Villa Reynolds
Q: Santa Rosa
R: Mar del Plata
S: Bahia Blanca
T: Comodoro Rivadavia
U: Rio Gallegos
V: Rio Grande

5

Argentine Air Forces

The following notes are an estimate compiled from several sources. Main sources, to which we record our gratitude, are Adrian J. English; and John M. Andrade's *Latin-American Military Aviation*, published 1982 by Midland Counties Publications (Aerophile) Ltd., 24 The Hollow, Earl Shilton, Leicester.

The **Fuerza Aerea Argentina** is organised in four Commands: Air Operations, Air Regions, Material and Personnel. The Comando de Operaciones Aereas consists of:

I Brigada Aerea (BAM El Palomar, BA)

The transport organisation, including:
STAM—Military Air Transport Service —with I, II and possibly III Escuadron de Transporte: Lockheed C-130, IA.50 Guarani II, Boeing 707.
LADE—State Air Lines—with Fokker F.27 and F.28, and DHC.6 Twin Otter.

I Bda. may also have under command the fixed- and rotary-winged transport aircraft of 1 Escuadron Antartico, based in Cordoba province.

II Brigada Aerea (BAM Gen. Justo de Urquiza, Parana, Entre Rios province)

I Escuadron de Bombardeo	—BAC Canberra B.62 and T.64
I Escuadron Fotografico	—IA.50 Guarani II, Lear Jet 35A

III Brigada Aerea (BAM Reconquista, Santa Fe)

II Escuadron de Exploracion y Ataque	—IA.58A Pucará Flights based at Stanley, Goose Green, Pebble Island, Fox Bay.
III Escuadron de Exploracion y Ataque	—IA.58A Pucará Pebble Island

IV Brigada Aerea (BAM El Plumerillo, Mendoza province)

I Escuadron de Caza-Bombardeo	—Douglas A-4P Skyhawk
II Esc. de Caza-Bombardeo	—Morane-Saulnier MS.760A Paris
III Esc. de Caza-Bombardeo	—Morane-Saulnier MS.760A Paris

aircraft. This figure evidently excluded the Pucarás, and (if truthful) might be taken to indicate that some of the A-4Ps had been cannibalised for spares. However, it is also possible that he was simply referring to the number of jet-powered combat aircraft that were available for action on the first day of the fighting, corresponding to perhaps 70 per cent of those on strength.

The country's navy (Armada Argentina) also had an air arm (Aviacion Naval Argentina: ANA), partly based on the 16,000-ton carrier *Veinticinco de Mayo* (formerly the Royal Netherlands Navy's *Karel Doorman*), which had operated up to a dozen A-4Qs (also based on the A-4B) and six Grumman S-2E Tracker piston-engined ASW aircraft, together with Sikorsky S-61D-4 (SH-3D) Sea King helicopters. Ironically, Britain had fought hard to sell ANA some Harriers to supersede the A-4Qs, and in 1969 one of these V/STOL aircraft had been demonstrated aboard the *Veinticinco de Mayo* during her delivery from Holland to Argentina, just after the carrier visited Portsmouth for catapult trials.

However, these marketing efforts did not bear fruit, ANA deciding instead to purchase a batch of

V Brigada Aerea (BAM Gen. Pringles, Villa Reynolds, San Luis province)

IV Esc. de Caza-Bombardeo	—Douglas A-4P Skyhawk
V Esc. de Caza-Bombardeo	—Douglas A-4P Skyhawk

VI Brigada Aerea (BAM Tandil, BA)

II Esc. de Caza	—IAI Dagger
III Esc. de Caza	—IAI Dagger

VII Brigada Aerea (BAM Dr. Mariano Moreno, Moron, BA)

I Escuadron de Exploracion y Ataque	—Hughes 500M, Bell UH-1H

VIII Brigada Aerea (BAM Dr. Mariano Moreno, Moron, BA)

I Esc. de Caza ('de Intercepción')	—Dassault-Breguet Mirage IIIEA/DA

IX and X Brigada Aerea were in process of formation at time of campaign.

The **Comando de Aviacion del Ejercito**—Army Aviation Command—is believed to be organised into General Aviation Support Company 601 operating a range of light fixed-wing types, and Combat Aviation Battalion 601 operating a range of helicopters. (All Argentine Army units which fall under direct Army command, rather than Corps or Brigade commands, are designated '601'.)

The **Comando de Aviacion Naval** is organised in six Escuadras Aeronavales—Naval Air Groups or Wings—and those important to the Falklands campaign were as follows:

3ªEscuadra Aeronaval (BAN Comandante Espora, Puerto Belgrano)

2ªEscuadrilla Aeronaval de Caza y Ataque	—Dassault Super Etendard
3ªEsdla.A.de Caza y Ataque	—Douglas A-4Q Skyhawk
1ªEsdla.A.de Helicopteros	—Sud Alouette III, Westland Lynx
2ªEsdla.A.de Helicopteros	—Sikorsky S.61D-4
3ªEsdla.A.de Prop.Gen.	—Beechcraft Queen Air or King Air

4ªEscuadra Aeronaval (BAN Punta del Indio or Ushuaia—sources differ)

1ªEsdla.A.de Ataque	—Aermacchi MB.326GB, MB.339A
4ªEsdla.A.de Prop.Gen.	—Beechcraft T-34C

14 Dassault-Breguet Super Etendard conventional attack aircraft, to be armed with the AM.39 Exocet anti-shipping missile. At the outbreak of hostilities, reports indicated that only five of these aircraft had been delivered, and that no operations had taken place from the carrier. In making the case for the Argentine purchase of Sea Harriers, British Aerospace had predicted that the ship's catapults would be incapable of launching the Super Etendard at full gross weight; now the truth of this claim seemed likely to be investigated with the whole world looking on.

In addition to its carrier-borne strike and ASW aircraft, ANA had recently purchased ten Aermacchi MB.339 advanced training aircraft, which could also be employed in close support missions, as could its Beech T-34C turboprop trainers. In addition, three ex-US Navy Lockheed SP-2H Neptune piston-engined maritime reconnaissance aircraft were available from their normal duties in the Antarctic. Argentina's ASW capability was still in the course of expansion; orders had been placed for Westland Lynx Mk 23 and 87, two Mk 23s having been delivered for use on Type

42 and Meko Type 360 warships. The first Mk 87 made its maiden flight at Yeovilton during the conflict.

Army Aviation (Aviacion del Ejercito) had a mixed fleet with a large helicopter element. Aircraft on strength included three Aeritalia G.222 tactical transports, two Boeing-Vertol CH-47C helicopters (of which FAA also had three), nine Agusta A.109s, seven Bell Jet Rangers, 20 Bell UH-1H 'Hueys' (six more served with FAA) and 12 Aerospatiale SA.330 Pumas (three more being operated by ANA).

In projecting air power into the area of the Falklands, Argentina had three main bases with runways of at least 7,000ft. (2,135m) within 500nm (925km) of the islands: Rio Grande, Rio Gallegos, and Comodoro Rivadavia. On the Falklands there was only one tarmac runway: the 4,200ft. (1,280m) strip at Stanley. Some 148ft. (45m) wide, it was built directly on rock, with hardcore filling the depressions in the natural surface. Although too short for the Mirages and A-4s, it could take a

V/STOL muscle on the flight deck of HMS *Hermes*. **Two Harrier GR.3s are at the front of this line-up, the nearest with a BL.755 cluster bomb visible on the outboard pylon. Four Sea Harrier FRS.1s are visible in the background, repainted grey overall with black numbers on the intakes. Appalling weather like this had surprisingly little effect on serviceability. (MoD)**

moderately well-loaded C-130 and various lighter transport aircraft, as well as close support aircraft such as the Pucará and MB.339. In addition, there were 20 or 30 grass airstrips of around 2,000ft. (610m) in length, which had been constructed to provide light aircraft links with the various settlements. Designed from the outset for anti-guerilla operations from general aviation strips, the Pucará was well suited to dispersal to such sites, although practical considerations such as refuelling, re-arming, maintenance and protection appear to have limited the regular use of grass airfields to those at Goose Green and Pebble Island.

In assessing the potential air threat to the British Task Force as it approached the Falklands, it was apparent that, provided the Argentine carrier could be bottled up in port by the Royal Navy's nuclear-powered submarines, then the principal danger was the Mirage family and the land-based A-4s. Computing performance from sales brochures, a Mirage with two 375-Imp.gal. (1,700-litre) tanks can deliver two 1,000lb (454kg) Mk 83 bombs over a radius of 500nm (925km), with the last ten per cent of that distance flown at low level to confuse AAW defences.

Similarly, an A-4P with two 250-Imp.gal. (1,135-litre) tanks on the wing pylons could carry four 500lb (227kg) Mk 82 bombs on the centre-line, and attack over a similar radius in the same mission profile. On the other hand, the Super Etendard is credited with an anti-shipping strike radius of only 350nm (650km) in a mission of unspecified profile. If accurate, this indicated that a land-based attack by this aircraft using Exocet against the Task Force was unlikely, unless the FAA agreed to refuel these naval aircraft using its KC-130H tankers (difficult, because of minimum airspeed considerations), or unless they could refuel from 'buddy-packs' mounted on other Super Etendards of A-4s.

In summary, Mirages, A-4s, and flight-refuelled Super Etendards could be expected to attack the Task Force as it approached the Falklands, but the brochure figures for radius of action left little in hand. In particular, it was clear that if the Mirage used its afterburner in combat it would probably not have sufficient fuel to return to base, hence Argentina had little prospect of winning air superiority over the Falklands. The FAA could only attack British surface vessels and ground forces, and

hope that the carriers would be exposed to attack by the Armada's Super Etendard and its AM.39. The handful of ageing Canberras could assist in medium-level attacks, but their slow speed made them easy meat for the Sea Harriers; they were virtually confined to night attacks in the hope that this would give them some chance of survival. Disregarding the Canberras, Argentina could thus support her forces on the Falklands with air power that was strong in regional terms, although fighters and attack aircraft had been emphasised at the expense of other categories, notably maritime patrol and tanker aircraft.

In preparing a long-range assault on the Argentine invaders, Britain had a larger and more balanced force-mix, but it had been optimised for use in co-operation with American and other NATO forces against Soviet Bloc forces in Europe and the North Atlantic. For many years past, little serious attention had been paid in British planning to the possibility of a major war 'out of theatre'. Mounting a solo operation in the South Atlantic brought out not only the logistic problems of distant actions, but also the dangers inherent in the assumption that any adversaries outside the NATO area would be third-rate powers, with military equipment to match.

Fortunately, Britain had Ascension Island roughly mid-way between home base and the scene of the action. Approximately 3,500nm (6,500km) from both the UK and the Falklands, Ascension was a convenient support facility, although diplomatically it was a touchy subject in the early

FAA Douglas A-4P Skyhawk at the time of delivery from America after conversion from A-4B standard. The first 25, ordered in 1966, were numbered 'C-201' to 'C-225'; another 25 ordered in 1970 were numbered 'C-226' to 'C-250'; and 25 more, in 1975, 'C-251' to 'C-275'. At least ten had been written off between delivery and the outbreak of hostilities, but the exact serviceable inventory in April 1982 is a matter of guesswork. The numbering of one aircraft 'C-313' in a clear photograph (see commentary Plate A3) is unexplained. (McDonnell Douglas via MARS)

days of the conflict before America came down on the British side, since Wideawake airbase is a US facility on a British island. In making use of Ascension, Britain had approximately 50 aircraft in the RAF's C-130 Hercules transport wing; but the wide-body Short Belfasts had been sold off, and had to be chartered from HeavyLift Cargo Airlines. Long-range operations would clearly require in-flight refuelling on a scale unprecedented in RAF experience, but the service's tanker strength was only 23 Victor K.2s, since the five planned VC10 K.2s and four Super VC10 K.3s were still in the process of conversion. However, the RAF's most serious shortcoming was the lack of AEW (airborne early warning) aircraft. The Nimrod AEW.3 had originally been scheduled to enter service early in 1982, but delays in developing its complex avionics had put back its initial operational capability by a whole year, removing it from possible participation in the South Atlantic.

For the long-range strike role from Ascension against the Falklands (with the implied threat that such missions could easily be switched to targets in Argentina), the Panavia Tornado GR.1 was not yet in squadron service, but the RAF still had three squadrons of Vulcans. Fitted with ECM (elec-

9

tronic countermeasures) in the form of ALQ-101 jammers and operating at night, these old aircraft on the brink of retirement could still perform usefully, delivering up to 21 1,000lb (454kg) bombs in a single attack. Less spectacular, though very useful RAF aircraft, included the VC10 C.1 passenger transport and the Boeing-Vertol CH-47C Chinook HC.1 medium-lift helicopter, of which the service had just acquired 33, each capable of carrying 44 troops or a 21,000lb (9,400kg) payload.

The RAF also had the McDonnell Douglas F-4 Phantom II, a multi-role fighter that had proved its value both in Vietnam and the Middle East. However, the F-4 is a conventional aircraft requiring a full-size runway, and having a radius of action corresponding to only a fraction of the distance from Ascension to the Falklands. It could defend Ascension, but the only means to provide air cover for the Task Force as it steamed south was the carrier-borne BAe (British Aerospace) Sea Harrier FRS.1.

First flown in August 1978, and delivered to the Royal Navy in June 1979, the Sea Harrier was the latest member of this world-beating V/STOL family of aircraft, fitted with Blue Fox nose radar, AIM–9 Sidewinder air-to-air missiles, and avionics revised to suit operation from a moving deck. Taking off from a 'ski-jump' without catapult assistance, and landing vertically without arrester gear, the Sea Harrier had made possible smaller, less expensive carriers. In naval exercises it had performed well in air defence, but it was far more effective when operating in conjunction with the US Navy's Grumman E-2C Hawkeye AEW aircraft. The Sea Harrier also excelled in close combat with conventional fighters capable of much higher speeds: kill ratios of 2:1 were claimed by the RN's No. 899 Sqn against F-5Es of the USAF 527th Aggressor Sqn, and the British aircraft was also claimed to have had the edge over the best of USAF fighters when No. 899 Sqn met F-15s and No. 800 Sqn met F-16s.

Nonetheless, even some of the Sea Harrier's most ardent admirers had reservations about its use in the South Atlantic. Aside from the fact that it had never been tested in war, its equipment was intended for vastly different missions. Its radar had been optimised for picking up a lone Soviet maritime patrol aircraft flying at medium altitude, not for detecting shoals of small aircraft skimming the waves or following the terrain of the islands. Its weapon delivery system was designed for attacks on ships, using radar range information, not for bombing ground targets that produce no radar response. Above all, there were simply not enough Sea Harriers to cope with wartime attrition rates. The RN had been allowed to buy only 34, of which

Sixteen A-4Bs were converted to A-4Q by McDonnell Douglas at Santa Monica for the Argentine Navy. They seem to have borne two different series of maintenance numbers since then; initially serials 0654 to 0669 were coded '3-A-201' to '3-A-216', but with a transfer to the 3ªEscuadrilla—see orbat —they bear '3-A-301' to '3-A-316'. At least five were written off before the Falklands campaign. The carrier *Veinticino de Mayo* **certainly did not launch them during her brief cruise of early May, but four were lost during missions over the TEZ from FAA bases in the south. This photo shows the delivery scheme. (McDonnell Douglas via MARS)**

two were still being built, one had crashed, and others were required in the UK for pilot training and for trials installations for new armament and equipment.

One possible way to strengthen the naval V/STOL force and to reduce attrition of Sea Harriers (each of which would take 30 months to replace) was to bring in the Harrier GR.3s of the RAF's No. 1(F) Sqn. Normally based at Wittering, this unit is part of a mobile force tasked with reinforcing NATO's flanks and dealing with overseas defence problems such as that of Belize. At present the RAF operates 12 Harriers as No. 1 Sqn, and 36 others in West Germany as Nos. 3 and 4 Sqn at Gütersloh. Starting in 1986, these aircraft in Germany will be replaced by the Harrier GR.5, i.e. a modified McDonnell Douglas AV-8B with final assembly by British Aerospace at Kingston. Surplus GR.3s will be returned to Wittering, where the Harrier force is expected to peak at around 50 aircraft, some of which will be refitted to extend their useful life to the end of the century. It is thus clear that on present plans the RAF will have more GR.3s in the late 1980s than it can operate.

Unfortunately, there were problems in using the GR.3 to supplement the Sea Harrier: it does not have the anti-corrosion modifications of the RN aircraft, it has no Sidewinder provisions, and its inertial platform was not intended for alignment

Argentina's seven C-130E/H Hercules transports, operating with the STAM in I Brigada Aerea, must have flown long hours to transport the bulk of the enemy garrison to the islands in the weeks before the Task Force's arrival off the Falklands. At least one of these aircraft was turned into a makeshift bomber; a mission on 31 May rolled bombs out the tail-ramp, which bounced off a ship without detonating—though one must pay tribute to the extraordinary feat of hitting anything at all by such a method. A second mission, perhaps by the same aircraft, paid the price of over-confidence when it was brought to a terminal conclusion by a Sea Harrier on 1 June. (via MARS)

(i.e. for levelling and north-seeking) on a moving deck. It should be added that No. 1 Sqn pilots had had no training whatever in naval operations. Notwithstanding these difficulties, the RAF's GR.3s could substitute for the Sea Harrier if necessary, and could well improve effectiveness in the close support role, if only because No. 1 Sqn pilots were trained for that mission.

Turning to rotary-wing aircraft, the RN was reasonably well equipped for ASW work, with the Westland Sea King HAS.5, Lynx HAS.2, and the older Wasp HAS.1; and for transporting men and equipment in the Sea King HC.4 and Wessex HU.5, although the service had nothing to compare with the RAF's Chinook. The Army Air Corps' best helicopter was the Lynx AH.1, but this was being delivered to serve in the anti-tank role in Germany, replacing the SS.11-armed Scout AH.1. The service also have a large number of Gazelle AH.1s operating in the reconnaissance and casualty-

Argentine Canberra B62, maintenance number 'B-101', in its delivery scheme of olive camouflage over dull grey. The wing markings were painted rather smaller in 1982, but in essentials this scheme still applies. See Plate A2. (via Mars)

evacuation roles. Scouts and Gazelles also equipped the Royal Marines' 3rd Commando Brigade Air Sqn (CBAS).

In summary, Britain possessed a reasonably large and well-balanced force of aircraft; but there was no way to provide AEW capability around the Falklands, and no way that the Vulcans, Nimrods, and Hercules could function effectively without large-scale use of in-flight refuelling, hence RAF tanker resources would be overstretched. In addition, the numbers of Sea Harriers available was severely restricted, and consequently air defence for the Task Force could become problematical if the fighting were to persist for a long time.

The Preparations

Once the British Government had decided to send a task force to free the Falklands, preparations went ahead at a staggering pace. Men and equipment were hurriedly loaded on board ship (occasionally on the wrong ship, and in the wrong order), and the main carrier group sailed from Portsmouth only three days after the Argentine invasion.

The force was led by the carriers HMS *Hermes* and *Invincible*, with respectively 12 and six Sea Harriers, all of which had flown from RNAS Yeovilton with AIM–9 Sidewinders in place on the outboard wing pylons. The operation (code-named Operation 'Corporate') proceeded so quickly that two aircraft had to join *Invincible* as it steamed down the Channel, bringing the total Sea Harrier force to 20. However, it still gave cause for concern that, once in the South Atlantic, Britain's fixed-wing aircraft would be outnumbered 10:1 by Argentina's Mirages, A-4s and Pucarás.

The normal fixed-wing complement of an *Invincible*-class carrier is five aircraft; on this occasion the ship carried sixty per cent more Sea Harriers, No. 801 Sqn having been enlarged by aircraft taken from the headquarters unit, No. 899 Sqn. Similarly, No. 800 Sqn aboard HMS *Hermes* was strengthened by other Sea Harriers from No. 899 Sqn, and the carrier's air wing was later to be joined by four aircraft from the newly formed No. 809 Sqn, in addition to Harrier GR.3s. *Invincible* also received four aircraft from No. 809 Sqn, but no GR.3s.

The Royal Navy's helicopter force consisted of four basic types, spread throughout the Task Force. Westland Sea Kings were represented by five HAS.2s of No. 824 Sqn on the RFAs (Royal Fleet Auxiliaries) *Fort Grange* and *Olmeda*, and ten of No. 825 Sqn transported on the container ship *Atlantic Causeway*; 14 HC.4s of No. 846 Sqn on *Hermes* and the assault ship *Fearless*; nine HAS.5s of No. 820 Sqn on *Invincible*, and nine of No. 826 Sqn on *Hermes*. Three further Sea Kings were sent out later as battle casualty replacements on the container ships *Atlantic Causeway* and *Contender Bezant*. The Westland Wessex force consisted of two HAS.3s of No. 737 Sqn, one each on the County class destroyers *Antrim* and *Glamorgan*; ten HU.5s of No. 845 Sqn on Ascension Island and various RFAs, 16 more on the *Atlantic Causeway* and the helicopter support ship *Engadine*, and 12 of No. 848 Sqn on the *Atlantic Conveyor* and the RFAs. Some 14 HAS.5s went out as battle casualty replacements on the *Atlantic Causeway* and *Astronomer* (another container ship). The 22 Westland Lynx HAS.2s of No. 815 Sqn were carried by destroyers and frigates. Finally, 11 Westland Wasp HAS.1s equipped some frigates, HMS *Endurance*, and STUFT (ships taken up from trade).

The helicopters of the Army Air Corps and the Royal Marine Commandos are conveniently discussed together, since the two services use the same types of aircraft, the Army providing those for the Commandos from its own buy of helicopters. The Army also trains Royal Marine pilots and crewmen, and the technicians of REME (Royal Electrical and Mechanical Engineers) who maintain the aircraft. The first of these units to leave for the Falklands was the 3rd Commando Brigade Air Squadron, taking all its six Scout AH.1s, and nine of its 12 Gazelle AH.1s, which were distributed between the various LSLs (landing ship, logistics) to reduce the possibility of losses due to enemy action in transit. The 3rd CBAS was followed by the Army's No. 656 Sqn, normally based at Netheravon, which took its full establishment of six Gazelles and six Scouts. Deployment took place in two groups, the first as a section of three Scouts

A Royal Navy lieutenant pilot of No.800 Sqn. climbs into his Sea Harrier FRS.1 on the deck of HMS *Hermes*. **Compare details of helmet and suit with Plate H; and see commentary on Plates B and C for notes on combat colour scheme applied to the Sea Harriers on their way south. (MoD)**

which left with the Parachute Regiment, and the second comprising the three remaining Scouts and the six Gazelles with the 5th Infantry Brigade.

For Operation 'Corporate' a number of modifications were made to the Army and Royal Marine helicopters. Most of the changes took the form of off-the-shelf modification kits that were held in readiness for any emergency, but were not incorporated in the aircraft in peacetime because of the weight penalties involved. Only one new Gazelle modification—the provision for Matra rocket pods with 68mm SNEB rockets—was specifically for the Falklands operation. It resulted from a Royal Marines request for equipment to provide smoke cover as an emergency screen for forward troops. It was not the intention to convert these reconnaissance helicopters into gunships, nor were they ever used as such in the South Atlantic. Typical of the speed of the whole operation, SNEB rockets were test-fired from a Gazelle on Easter

HMS *Invincible* **zig-zags through the South Atlantic, to minimise the threat of enemy submarines. Two Harriers (background) disturb the rainwater on her flight deck before take-off; four more are visible, from her total complement of ten. The Sea Kings are conspicuously absent, presumably on ASW duty. The blast deflector behind** *Invincible's* **bow Sea Dart launchers is heavily marked—how recently the SAMs had been launched is hard to tell. (MoD)**

Monday (12 April), and the modification was cleared for fitment to begin on the Tuesday.

A total of 16 Gazelles were modified by REME's No. 70 Aircraft Workshop at Middle Wallop for No. 3 CBAS and No. 656 Sqn AAC, to incorporate SNEB provisions, armour plate (as used on Gazelles in Northern Ireland), radio altimeters, IFF (identification friend/foe) transponder, and a main rotor head that allowed the blades to be folded for carriage on ship. Ironically, the original Gazelle rotor head had had folding blades, but in the course of uprating the transmission this capability had been deleted, and now had to be restored specifically for this operation. Other changes included the installation of flotation gear for the shipboard operation of some helicopters.

Some Royal Marine Gazelles were fitted at Ascension with flexibly-mounted GPMGs (general purpose machine guns), using mountings produced for the Volvo BV202 snow vehicle. The helicopter's port door was removed to give a wide field of fire, and to allow escape in a crash-landing. A load-carrying tube mounted transversely through the fuselage provided four hardpoints, the inboard ones for six-tube Matra rocket pods, and the outboard ones for flares to illuminate landing sites at night.

In the case of Britain's fixed-wing aircraft, some modifications were made in the UK, others were introduced later, and most were a combined effort by services and industry, both working flat-out. The Sea Harrier required comparatively little in the way of changes, although the AIM-9L version of Sidewinder had to be rushed into service (it was already in the inventory and had been cleared for the Sea Harrier) to provide an all-aspect air-to-air attack capability. Earlier Sidewinder variants, notably the AIM-9G/H, were also employed. In addition, the aircraft was quickly cleared to use 2in. (5cm) air-to-ground rockets, and the RAF's Hunting BL.755 cluster bomb. A software change was made to the WAC (weapon-aiming computer) to permit loft bombing from an offset radar IP (initial point). The aircraft was also cleared for increased take-off weight from a ski-jump, and for the use of a pair of 330-Imp.gal. (1,500-litre) ferry tanks. In view of the threat posed by Argentine radar-directed AAA (anti-aircraft artillery) and guided missiles, an internal system of chaff/flare dispensing was developed in the UK using off-the-shelf American equipment, although this came into operational use only late in the conflict.

The RAF's Harrier GR.3 required more modifications, since its airframe, engine and systems had never been intended for operation from aircraft carriers. Nor had the aircraft been intended for air defence duties, although the US Marines' AV-8A version can carry Sidewinders on the outboard pylons. However, the initial need envisaged for GR.3s in Operation 'Corporate' was to replace Sea Harriers in the air defence role as wartime attrition reduced their numbers, and therefore a modification was designed to allow the armament wiring to the outboard pylons of the GR.3s to be used for Sidewinder, although this (unlike the wiring of the Sea Harrier) then made it impossible to use bombs or rocket pods on those pylons. Some firing trials were quickly mounted at the Aberporth range in North Wales, and the GR.3 was cleared to fire Sidewinder by 3 May, when the aircraft of No.1(F) Sqn deployed to Ascension. Other armament developments included clearance for the 1,000lb (454kg) Paveway LGB (laser-guided bomb).

As mentioned earlier, the Ferranti FE541 inertial navigation system of the GR.3 is not intended for alignment on a moving deck; when it came to developing the Sea Harrier the aircraft manufacturer had adopted a completely different system—a twin-gyro platform and Doppler radar—which avoided this problem. To operate GR.3s from *Hermes* it was not possible to fit a new nav-attack system; instead Ferranti produced a trolley-mounted inertial platform (FINRAE: Ferranti inertial rapid alignment equipment) to act as an on-the-deck reference system, giving the aircraft reasonably accurate data for platform levelling and true north alignment before each sortie. Once again, this equipment was available and installed on *Hermes* in an incredibly short time, the final software for FINRAE being transmitted to the ship at sea via satellite communications link.

To reduce salt water corrosion of airframe and engines, some of the special sealing and drainage techniques developed for the Sea Harrier were used by the RAF in preparing the GR.3s, and all the aircraft (including all but the largest helicopters) transported to the Task Force on the deck of the *Atlantic Conveyor* were covered in plastic bags

Three RAF Hercules C.1s at Wideawake airbase on Ascension Island. The nearest, XV295, is still being unloaded. Rapid turnaround was essential because of the limited ramp-area available. Note satellite tracking station on hill in background. (MoD)

specially manufactured in the course of a few days by Driclad of Sittingbourne in Kent. Other modifications for the GR.3 included a radar transponder (already fitted to the Sea Harrier) to assist the carriers in locating their aircraft when returning from a sortie. This transponder accounts for the small bulge and blade antenna below the nose of GR.3s photographed on *Hermes*.

Turning to the subject of how the GR.3s were deployed to the Falklands, it may be noted that 12 Sea Harriers had left the UK on 5 April with *Hermes* and eight with *Invincible*. On 16 April the Task Force left Ascension, and arrived in the TEZ (Total Exclusion Zone) at the end of the month. On 30 April eight Sea Harriers of No.809 flew from UK to Ascension, to join the *Atlantic Conveyor*, which had steamed from Britain on 23 April. On 3 May three waves of GR.3s took off from St Mawgan for Ascension, to be tankered by Victor K.2s (as were the six Sea Harriers). The details of the operation have not been published, but it seems likely that there were four GR.3s in each wave, one of the four being of a spare aircraft that turned back home after the first refuelling had been successfully completed. The remaining nine proceeded toward Ascension, but at least one hook-up failed, and the GR.3 diverted to an airfield (possibly Dakar) to continue the flight later. In any event, by 5 May eight GR.3s were available on Ascension, and of these six took off to land vertically on the container ship, as did the six Sea Harriers. The *Atlantic Conveyor* had been given a 50ft. × 8oft. (15 × 25m) landing pad at the forward end of the deck, the remainder of the deck

A Victor K.2 of No.57 Sqn. refuels a specially modified Hercules C.1 transport—a process repeated many times during the Falklands campaign. In-flight refuelling allowed the Hercules to become airborne with a heavier payload, without the usual trade-off in range. Special long-range missions were also flown by the Hercules to insert teams of SAS/SBS off South Georgia, and the mainland of South America. (MoD)

forming an open hangar between three layers of containers arranged as sidewalls.

Two GR.3s remained behind at Ascension to provide air cover for this vital base, later being joined by the aircraft that had been delayed in Africa, and ultimately being replaced by Phantom FGR.2s of No. 29 Sqn on 24 May. The Sea Harriers and GR.3s on the *Atlantic Conveyor* transferred to the two carriers on 18 and 19 May, four Sea Harriers and all six GR.3s landing on *Hermes* (the first time most of the RAF pilots had even *seen* an aircraft carrier!) and the remaining four naval aircraft on *Invincible*. Five GR.3s flew the 9hr. 15min. ferry from the UK to Ascension at the end of May, bringing the total at Wideawake to eight, of which two flew to *Hermes* on 1 June; four left on the *Contender Bezante* two days later (arriving after the Argentine surrender); and two flew to *Hermes* on the 8th.

For this remarkable ferry flight from Ascension to the Task Force the GR.3s' inertial systems were extremely carefully aligned prior to take-off, and they were escorted most of the way by Victor tankers which provided navigation updates. However, for the final 800nm (1,500km) each pair of GR.3s was alone, until picked up by *Hermes*' radar and met by Sea Harriers which escorted them to the ship.

The initial force of 20 Sea Harriers had left the UK so hurriedly that there had been no time for additional air combat training, although this V/STOL aircraft family had previously been tested successfully against virtually every high performance fighter in the West, and against attack aircraft such as the Douglas A-4 and the Etendard. Nonetheless, experience against the Mirage III family was limited; and by the time the two carriers had reached Ascension further air combat trials had been carried out (courtesy of the French services) against any remaining aircraft types that might have posed a threat in the Falklands area.

During the voyage south a great deal of work was done on the Sea Harriers to prepare them for combat, notably on the Ferranti Blue Fox radars, which initially gave inconsistent performance, but went into battle more reliable than ever before as a result of considerable 'fine tuning'.

The Fleet Air Arm pilots had long been aware that the peacetime paint-scheme of gloss dark sea grey upper surfaces and white undersides was a relatively high visibility scheme, and knew that in war it would be replaced by a pale grey scheme similar to that being introduced on some RAF fighters. In the event, *Hermes*' 12 Sea Harriers were repainted by hand *en route*, covering the white underside with the upper surface dark sea grey, painting out the white ring of the roundel with blue (as on RAF aircraft), and painting side numbers in matt black. The fancy squadron markings on the fins were also painted over. Sea Harriers coming out later were painted at Yeovilton in matt light and 'Barley' grey overall, similar to the RAF scheme for Phantoms. In practice, it was to be found that the dark sea grey aircraft were difficult to see at low level, and that the light grey aircraft 'disappeared' at high level.[1] The GR.3s retained their standard 'toned down' tactical camouflage.

The modifications to the Harrier family have been discussed in some detail because of the aircraft's critical role in the South Atlantic. However, several other aircraft types needed major modifications, notably for in-flight refuelling to support long-range operations. For example, the Vulcan bomber in its early service years had a refuelling probe, retained on the Vulcan SR.2s of No.27 Sqn but no longer a standard item on the Vulcan B.2; in most cases the probe had been removed to be stored on base or returned to British Aerospace. For the bombing of Stanley airport and attacks on radar installations, these probes had to be recovered and checked for serviceability prior to refitting.

The maritime reconnaissance Vulcans (SR.2s of No.27 Sqn at Scampton) had long been flying with underwing pylons to accommodate additional sensors: these pylons were fitted to at least one Vulcan B.2 (XM597) to carry the AGM-45A Shrike anti-radiation missile. In addition, the decision was taken to modify a batch of six Vulcans for the tanker role (thus becoming K.2s), to substitute for the Victor K.2, which was in short supply. Known at BAe, Manchester as 'The 50-Day Wonder', the project was first discussed at Woodford late on 30 April, received its go-ahead on 4 May, flew on 18 June, and was awarded its C(A) Release on 23 June, when the first was delivered to No.50 Sqn at Waddington. In the Vulcan K.2 the HDU (hose/drum unit) of the flight refuelling system is housed in a rear fuselage bay previously allocated to ECM (electronic counter-measures), allowing an additional cylindrical fuel tank to be placed in the weapons bay.

Another aircraft requiring a flight-refuelling probe was the Nimrod maritime reconnaissance aircraft, the demand being passed from MoD (Ministry of Defence) to BAe on 13 April. Under

normal circumstances such modifications would take many months: yet the first of 13 Nimrod MR.2P (XV229) made its maiden flight only two weeks later, on 27 April, using a probe removed from a Vulcan (XM603) that had been handed over to BAe as a museum piece. In addition to the probe over the flight deck, the 2P is distinguished by a strake under the rear fuselage to counter-balance the effect of the nose probe on directional stability. Following three encounters with an Argentine Boeing 707-320B (a military VIP transport used in the maritime reconnaissance role), some Nimrods were fitted with Sidewinders on pylons intended for the Martel anti-radiation missile, but (by coincidence) the 707 was not encountered again. Other armament changes included the carriage of the Stingray torpedo and, later, the Harpoon anti-ship missile.

The standard Hercules C.1 and the stretched C.3 undoubtedly played a major role in supporting British forces in the South Atlantic, but at least seven C-130s were converted for long-range operations with two extra fuel tanks in the centre fuselage and flight-refuelling probes. To avoid the performance incompatibility between Victor tanker and Hercules, four C-130s have since been

The Fortuna Glacier, South Georgia: four snow-suited SAS troopers return to the scene of the loss of two Wessex HU.5 helicopters in earlier attempts to extract the special forces party in the middle of a blizzard, presumably to salvage valuable equipment. The successful rescue of the SAS men and the stranded aircrew earned Lt.Cdr. Ian Stanley, pilot of HMS *Antrim's* **Wessex HAS.3 the Distinguished Service Order. (MoD)**

[1] A Task Force pilot later reported that intercepted FAA radio traffic referred to the darker grey Harriers as the 'Black Death', a dramatic choice of words which tends to confirm the efficiency of both colour scheme and aircraft.

17

converted to the tanker role in a six-week programme by Marshalls of Cambridge and A & AEE (Aircraft and Armament Experimental Establishment) at Boscombe Down. The first Hercules tanker arrived at Ascension early in August. In this conversion, the rear ramp is permanently closed, and the HDU located on the floor, streaming the drogue through an aperture in the ramp. In addition to the normal fuel tanks, four cylinders containing a total of 28,000lb (12,700kg) of extra fuel are mounted in the cabin. However, during the conflict all British tankering in the area was performed by the Victors, which arrived in Ascension on 18 April. Some of these aircraft were converted to the maritime radar reconnaissance role, with modified radar, cameras (in some of these aircraft) and different navigation systems. An inertial navigator was fitted initially, but this was later replaced by Omega navigation, also used by the Hercules, Nimrods, and Vulcans.

The War in the Air

The initial role of aircraft in the conflict was to move men and materiel. Argentina (having lost a Puma and an Alouette to Royal Marines small arms fire in the conquest of South Georgia) used helicopters to provide transport for small sections to remote settlements, while fixed-wing aircraft brought in thousands of men and many tons of equipment to the islands. Meanwhile, the British Task Force sailed down the Channel, with last-minute provisions being flown on board by the RN's Sea Kings of No.706 Sqn (the training unit for the HAS.5) and the RAF's Chinook HC.1s of No.18 Sqn.

Even before the Task Force had sailed, the RAF's

air transport effort had started, with the first eight C-130s leaving for Ascension on 3 April, while a VC10 of No.10 Sqn left Brize Norton to collect the Falklands' governor and his party from Uruguay. By the middle of the month Ascension's Wideawake airbase was well on the way to becoming one of the busiest airports in the world: it peaked at approximately 400 aircraft movements per day, compared to its normal 40 per month! A Marconi Martello transportable early warning radar system was set up to safeguard against Argentine attack, and a terminal control area established to a radius of 200nm (370km). Communications and meteorological facilities were provided respectively by the RAF Tactical Communications Wing (working alongside No.30 Signals Regiment, Royal Corps of Signals) and No.38 Group Mobile Met Unit.

One restriction on the use of Wideawake was the limited area of hardstanding available, providing space for a maximum of 25–30 aircraft, depending on the type-mix. Priority had to be given to the Victor tankers of Nos.55 and 57 Sqns, up to 16 of which had to be based there. In addition, throughout most of the conflict, there were smaller numbers of C-130s, Nimrods, VC10s, Vulcans, Harriers, and Phantoms. Search and rescue facilities were provided by an RAF Sea King HAR.3 of No.202 Sqn, assisted by Nimrods.

The Task Force left Ascension on 16 April, and four days later the first reconnaissance mission by a camera-equipped Victor was flown over South Georgia to pave the way for repossession of the island. The flight lasted 14hrs. 40 minutes. On the same day Vulcan crews started training for conventional bombing. On 21 April the first airdrop to the Task Force was made by a C-130, and a Sea Harrier intercepted and turned away an Argentine Boeing 707-320B evidently carrying out a search for the British ships.

In view of the possible threat to the Task Force from four Argentine submarines a major ASW effort was essential, and nonstop patrols were therefore flown by RN helicopters, day and night, for three months from the time that the ships left Ascension. The units involved were *Invincible*'s No.820 Sqn and *Hermes*' No.826 Sqn with Sea King HAS.5s, which had been employed at Ascension along with the Sea King HC.4s of No.846 Sqn in a

Sea King HAS.5 being hooked-on to more supplies for the flagship, HMS *Hermes*, on the deck of the Royal Fleet Auxiliary *Fort Austin*. The huge task of cross-decking and re-supply during the various operations by the rapidly-mounted Task Force forced even the HAS.5—the Royal Navy's most advanced anti-submarine helicopter—into the role of heavy-lift transport, and the ASW capability was stretched to the limit. (MoD)

Sea King HAS.5 being readied for flight aboard HMS *Hermes*. The workhorse of the Task Force, the Sea King's wide range of missions under all conditions of weather, visibility, and enemy presence led to inevitable losses, but its success was beyond question. (MoD)

Douglas A-4P Skyhawk 'C-210' of the FAA's V Brigada Aerea, in the colour scheme apparently borne by two squadrons of that formation at the outbreak of hostilities, but without the yellow tactical bands added later—see Plate D. The slight contrast between the grey and olive of the original camouflage can just be seen under the olive top coat. The last two digits of the maintenance number are repeated on the nosewheel door. (Adrian English)

massive cross-decking and restow programme. They were supplemented by Sea King HAS.2s of No.825 Sqn on the RFAs, with A Flight on *Olmeda*, C and G Flights on *Fort Grange*, and F Flight on *Fort Austin*, which had joined from Gibraltar.

The ASW sorties lasted up to four hours, initially using sonobouys in the deep water south of Ascension, then dunking sonar in the shallow waters of the TEZ (Total Exclusion Zone), where there were many contacts; some of these had depth charges or homing torpedoes expended on them, although the majority were probably not submarines. This need for a continuous ASW screen placed heavy demands on both aircraft and crews: one Sea King is calculated to have spent a third of one month airborne!

Ahead of the Task Force, the destroyers *Antrim* and *Glamorgan* (each with a Wessex HAS.3 of No.727 Sqn) had steamed south from Gibraltar at the beginning of April to rendezvous with a number of other ships and retake South Georgia. This 'mini task force' included the destroyer *Brilliant* (two Lynx HAS.2s of No.815 Sqn), the RFA *Tidespring* (two Wessex HU.5s of No. 845 Sqn), and the frigate *Plymouth* and ice patrol ship *Endurance* (each with a Wasp HAS.1 of No.829 Sqn). Reconnaissance parties were duly landed by the two Wessex HU.5s and *Antrim*'s HAS.3, but appalling weather forced their extraction, in the course of which both HU.5s crashed while attempting to take off in 'white-out' conditions (i.e. loss of visible horizon due to snow). Nonetheless, the Wessex HAS.3 (XP142) succeeded in rescuing the SAS party and the crews of both the other helicopters. A third helicopter loss occurred on 23 April, when a Sea King HC.4 of No.846 Sqn, carrying out a night vertical replenishment mission from *Hermes*, ditched in the sea. The pilot was rescued, but the crewman drowned.

It was the same Wessex HAS.3 (flown by Lt.Cdr. Stanley) which had rescued the men from the Fortuna Glacier that on 25 April attacked the Argentine submarine *Santa Fé*, which had been detected by *Antrim* some 5nm (9.3km) outward bound from Grytviken harbour. Seriously damaged by the helicopter's depth charges exploding under her stern glands, the *Santa Fé* was finished off by *Endurance*'s Wasp firing AS.12 wire-guided missiles. The submarine limped back into Grytviken and sank alongside the jetty. Later that day *Antrim*'s Wessex and *Brilliant*'s two Lynx landed Royal Marines, while the ships provided a firepower demonstration that cowed the Argentine garrison into submission.

Up to this point very few lives had been lost on either side, and it still seemed possible that a last-minute diplomatic solution might be found to the problem. However, Argentina refused to withdraw her forces; and so British preparations for landings on the Falklands went ahead. On 29 April the first Vulcans were deployed to Ascension, which by that stage had over half the RAF's Victor tanker force. The Argentine troops around Stanley were about to bear witness to the delivery of the maximum conventional ordnance load of one of the heaviest bombers in the world, operating over a radius that was to create a new record in the history of aerial bombardment. Beyond any immediate physical damage, the strike was clearly intended to bring home an important message to President Galtieri. The row of massive craters that was shortly to appear across the newly-designated 'Aerodromo Malvinas' could just as well be repeated on the operational airfields in the south of Argentina, and could devastate military installations in the north.

The Vulcan, XM607 of No.44 Sqn, with a crew from No.101 Sqn, took off from Ascension just after 2300hrs GMT on the evening of April 30. Its warload consisted of 21 general purpose 1,000lb (454kg) free-fall bombs—notwithstanding some imaginative Press accounts that it dropped the Hunting JP.233 airfield denial weapon (a munitions dispenser that is not dropped, but is retained on the aircraft, and in any case has never been applied to the Vulcan).

Flight-refuelled by Victors (reports suggest that ten tankers were required), the Vulcan reached Stanley airport at 0745 GMT (0345 local time) on the morning of 1 May. The bombs were dropped by reference to the aircraft's ground-mapping radar, in a single stick at approximately 30° to the runway, the classic line of attack to ensure at least one crater in its surface. One bomb hit the centre-line of the

runway, and the remainder marched on toward the airport facilities and aircraft parking area; the flashes of the explosions were clearly visible to the crew of the Vulcan, and the shock waves were felt through the aircraft structure. There was no evidence of defensive fire, and the crew transmitted their code-name 'Black Buck' to the Task Force to indicate completion of the strike as they began the long haul back to Ascension. The complete mission took almost 16 hours, the Vulcan landing back at 1445hrs GMT.

Since Pucarás and lightly-loaded C-130s could operate from half the length of the Stanley runway, and since it is practically impossible to make large craters in a runway built on solid rock (the bombs were later found to have only 'scabbed' the surface), it was never expected to close the airport completely. The principal aim was to deny its use to Argentine Mirages, A-4s and Super Etendards, and thus keep them operating at the limit of their radius. This objective was achieved with a combination of Vulcan and Harrier strikes. In addition, it was hoped to force the Argentines to disperse aircraft and supplies away from the main airhead by damaging parked aircraft and rendering the airport buildings unserviceable, and these aims were also achieved. There was always the possibility that A-4s or Super Etendards would be based at Stanley, using American-made hydraulic arrester gears; hence a continuing effort was necessary to disrupt aircraft operating areas. In the event, the Argentines never succeeded in landing fast jets on the airfield.

The Vulcan's night attack was followed by a low

Blurred but interesting photo of A-4P 'C-237' on operations during the war, with clustering ground crew.

Unlike 'C-313', the subject of colour plate A3, this A-4P Skyhawk displays a full set of IV Brigada Aerea nose markings on its olive and light grey camouflage scheme. The 'ship kill' tally appears to be in red.

level dawn strike against Stanley airfield and that at Goose Green by Sea Harriers from the Task Force, which had closed in to a position 90nm (167km) east of the islands. For all operational missions, the Sea Harrier and the RAF's GR.3 (which joined *Hermes* later in the month) carried 100-Imp.gal. (454-litre) drop-tanks on the inboard wing pylons and two 30mm Aden cannon pods under the fuselage, leaving the outboard wing pylons and the centre-line pylon for bombs, rockets, or missiles. For ground attack missions these three pylons were generally used for 1,000lb (454kg) GP bombs or Hunting BL.755 cluster weapons (single carriage in either case). The latter had been developed originally for anti-tank use, but also gave worthwhile effects over a large area against parked aircraft, radars, and AAA. On the occasion of the first strike other Sea Harriers flew as escorts in the air defence configuration, with an AIM–9L Sidewinder on each outboard pylon. No enemy aircraft were encountered, but ground fire was intense. Short Tigercat SAMs were also launched, but without success. To quote one pilot: 'It was like Fireworks Night: they were hosing it around everywhere!' Nonetheless, the only damage suffered was a bullet-hole in the fin of one Sea Harrier. The hole was cleaned up and patched with 'speed-tape', which might be described as heavy-duty aluminium kitchen foil with adhesive backing. The

RN's first real experience of battle damage took 3.5hrs to repair, but similar holes were patched over within 1.5hrs later in the conflict. For this first operation the RN established a line of SAR (search and rescue) helicopters out from the carriers, but thereafter this mission was left to the ASW Sea King screen with complete success.

Keeping up the pressure on the Argentines, that same afternoon warships from the Task Force closed in and bombarded Stanley airport. This finally provoked retaliation from the FAA, which sent over a number of Mirages at high level. These aircraft were intercepted by Sea Harriers, and what followed was probably the closest thing to a traditional dogfight to be seen in the Falklands conflict. The first air-to-air kill came at 1915hrs GMT, and the victor was Flt.Lt. Paul Barton of the RAF, flying a Sea Harrier of No.801 Sqn from *Invincible*. This engagement between two Sea Harriers and two Mirages began virtually head-on, but the RN pilots were soon positioned behind the enemy aircraft. Barton fired an AIM–9L at a range of approximately 1nm (1,850m), and the Mirage burst into a ball of flame. From descriptions of later combats, this fight appears to have been typical in several respects: a brief slashing encounter that ended as the Argentine aircraft fireballed. Few pilots survived a strike by the AIM–9L.

A second Mirage was probably destroyed that day by another RAF pilot, Flt.Lt. Bertie Penfold, who lined up behind one which had unsuccessfully fired an older-model Sidewinder AIM–9B at his wingman. Once again, the characteristic growl in the head-phones from the locked-on AIM–9L—a flight time of three or four seconds—and a large explosion. A third Mirage is believed to have been shot down by Argentine ground defences, and is listed in the UK as an 'own goal'.

Later that evening a flight of Canberras attempted to attack the British ships carrying out the bombardment. They approached at medium level, then descended to low altitude; but they too were intercepted by Sea Harriers, and turned and ran, one being shot down while the rest made their escape. This first day's combat had proved that the Sea Harriers could be positioned correctly by the controllers on the ships; that AIM–9L worked as advertised; and that the Royal Navy's training emphasis on air combat had been worthwhile.

It was probably in an attempt to rescue some of the aircrew shot down in that battle that Argentina sent two occan-going patrol craft into the TEZ, the *Alferez Sobral* and *Comodoro Somellera*. At about 0400hrs GMT on 3 May, in the middle of an inky-black night, one of these boats fired on an RN Sea King, which called for assistance from Lynxes based on destroyers in the area. Two were scrambled and engaged the boats from outside their 40mm gun range, using the brand-new BAc Sca Skua sea-skimming anti-FPB missile, which had been rushed to the South Atlantic before completing its acceptance trials. Three pairs of Sea Skuas were fired, and the 800-ton *Somellera* disappeared from the helicopters' radar, while the *Sobral* limped away badly damaged. Later in the conflict one more Sea Skua was fired, also scoring a direct hit.

Another sea-skimming missile was to have its operational debut on the afternoon of the next day, when HMS *Sheffield* was destroyed by a direct hit from one of a pair of Aérospatiale AM.39 Exocet missiles, fired from a range of about 5nm (7km) by one of three Super Etendard aircraft of the ANA's 2ᵃ Escuadrilla de Ataque. (At least one and possibly two Super Etendards carried 'buddy-packs' to refuel the Exocet-armed aircraft in transit.) Reports indicate that the other missile may have been decoyed by chaff, and that the successful round failed to explode. However, its remaining rocket fuel started fires which quickly spread thick smoke throughout the ship, and cut off power supplies to fire-fighting equipment. The destruction of a Type 42 destroyer by a single hit is evidence of Exocet's lethality; but it is noteworthy that the missile was fired against a radar blip in the hope that this would prove a worthwhile target, and that it happened to strike one of the most fire-prone areas of the ship.

Tuesday 4 May also saw the second Vulcan bombing raid on the Stanley airport area (reportedly by the same aircraft, but with a crew from No. 50 Sqn); and the first loss of a Sea Harrier in the conflict. The aircraft was shot down by ground fire while taking part in an attack on Goose

The Lynx helicopter and Sea Skua sea-skimming ASM proved a deadly combination in the South Atlantic. Numerous light vessels of the ANA made forays into the Total Exclusion Zone; after encountering the Lynx, a number failed to return to their home ports. A total of seven Sea Skuas were launched in anger, and all found their targets. This Lynx on the flight deck of *Hermes* **appears to carry only two rounds—half its full complement—and this may have been standard practice in the TEZ, to increase operational radius. (MoD)**

The five Super Etendards known to have been delivered to the ANA's 2ªEscuadrilla de Ataque before hostilities broke out, marked as '3-A-201' to '3-A-205'. See Plate F for marking details. (A M Dassault via MARS)

Green airfield from *Hermes*. Judging by Argentine film of the wreckage, a large-calibre warhead probably exploded in the integral wing fuel tank. The pilot, Lt.Cdr. Nick Taylor, was killed. Further Sea Harrier losses occurred on 6 May, when two aircraft from *Invincible* are believed to have collided in fog; both pilots, Lt.Cdr. John Eyton-Jones and Lt. William Curtis, were lost.

The fog persisted much of the time for the first three weeks of May, which reduced the level of flying activity on both sides. At times it was impossible to see across the decks of the carriers, and 100 per cent humidity was experienced for up to six days at a time. Nonetheless, at 1230 GMT on 9 May two Sea Harriers patrolling the TEZ sighted an Argentine fishing vessel, the *Narwal*, which had been shadowing the Task Force for some days. At that stage the aircraft flew CAP (combat air patrol) missions with a single 1,000lb (454kg) bomb on the centre-line pylon, and if no suitable target of opportunity appeared it was dropped on Stanley airfield 'to agitate the Argies'. One Sea Harrier hit the *Narwal* with a bomb, which failed to explode but killed one of the crew. The pilots then strafed the boat with 30mm cannon fire, and called up two

other Sea Harriers, which also raked it with shells. The crew abandoned ship and were picked up by RN helicopters, and the *Narwal* sank later. Also on 9 May, other Sea Harriers bombed military targets around Stanley and turned back an Argentine C-130 escorted by two Mirages.

On 12 May three waves of four A-4s attacked the Task Force, two of the aircraft being shot down. As was usual, these attacks came in the late afternoon, so that Argentine aircraft approaching from the west would have the setting sun behind them, while British attacks from the Task Force in the east were mainly at dawn. A Sea King HAS.5 ditched on 12 May due to a systems malfunction, an accident that was to be repeated six days later. At the time there was some concern expressed over the reliability of the Sea King, but these two accidents were not really surprising in view of the hours being flown.

Sea King HC.4s of No.846 Sqn played a major role in landing SAS troops for the raid on Pebble Island early in the morning of 15 May, resulting in the destruction of six Pucarás, one Short Skyvan, and other light aircraft, in addition to an important radar installation. There is also little doubt that an SAS operation was behind the landing in southern Chile of a Sea King HC.4 (ZA290) on 20 May, the aircraft subsequently being destroyed by its crew. On the following day one of the worst accidents of the conflict occurred, when an HC.4 ditched following a birdstrike (some accounts say an

Blurred but interesting photo of Super Etendard serial 0752, '3-A-202' of the ANA's 2ªEscuadrilla de Ataque, believed to have been taken at Rio Gallegos airbase. Just visible, as a white blur, is the 'buddy-pack' under the belly for in-flight refuelling of other aircraft—probably a vital factor in the success of the Exocet missions flown by this unit.

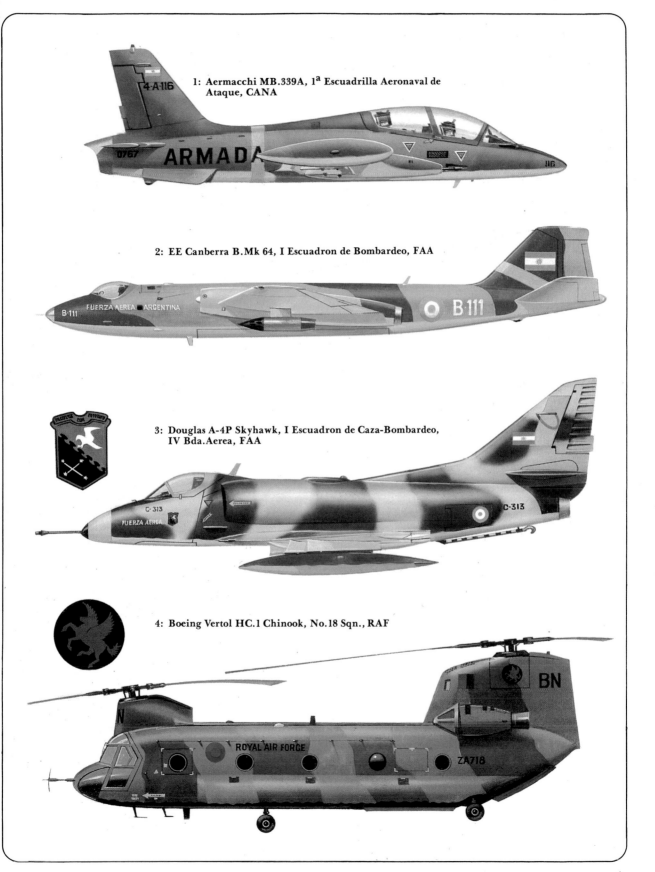

1: **Aermacchi MB.339A, 1ª Escuadrilla Aeronaval de Ataque, CANA**

2: **EE Canberra B.Mk 64, I Escuadron de Bombardeo, FAA**

3: **Douglas A-4P Skyhawk, I Escuadron de Caza-Bombardeo, IV Bda.Aerea, FAA**

4: **Boeing Vertol HC.1 Chinook, No.18 Sqn., RAF**

A

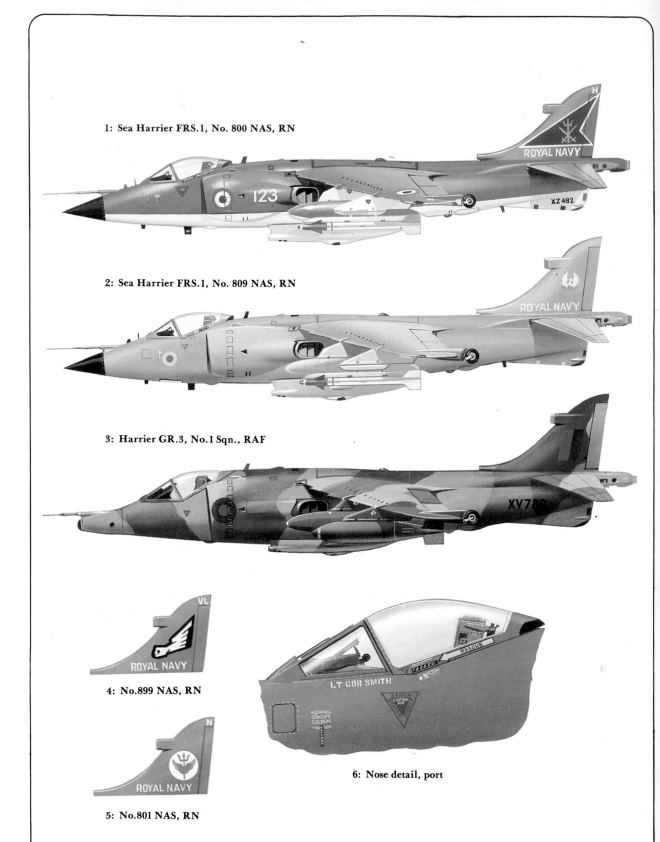

1: Sea Harrier FRS.1, No. 800 NAS, RN

2: Sea Harrier FRS.1, No. 809 NAS, RN

3: Harrier GR.3, No.1 Sqn., RAF

4: No.899 NAS, RN

5: No.801 NAS, RN

6: Nose detail, port

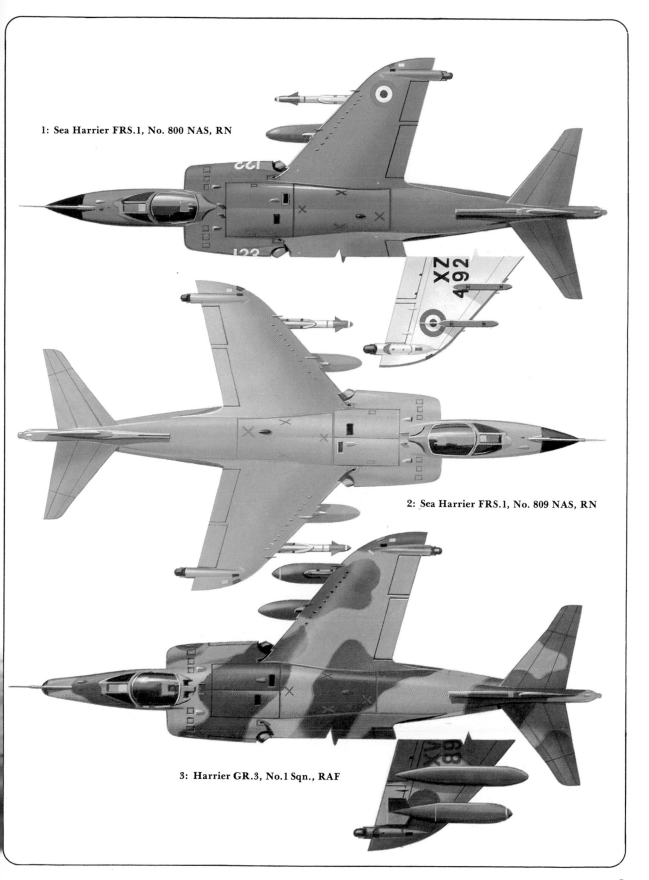

1: Sea Harrier FRS.1, No. 800 NAS, RN

2: Sea Harrier FRS.1, No. 809 NAS, RN

3: Harrier GR.3, No.1 Sqn., RAF

C

Douglas A-4P Skyhawk, V Brigada Aerea, Fuerza Aerea Argentina

V Brigada Aerea

D

Israel Aircraft Industries Dagger, VI Brigada Aerea, Fuerza Aerea Argentina

VI Brigada Aerea

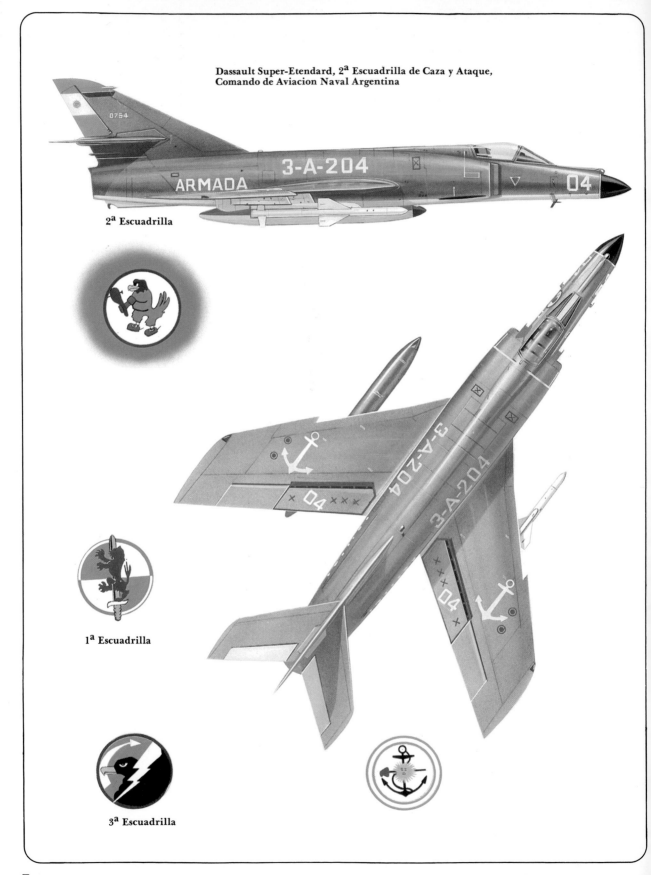

Dassault Super-Etendard, 2ª Escuadrilla de Caza y Ataque,
Comando de Aviacion Naval Argentina

2ª Escuadrilla

1ª Escuadrilla

3ª Escuadrilla

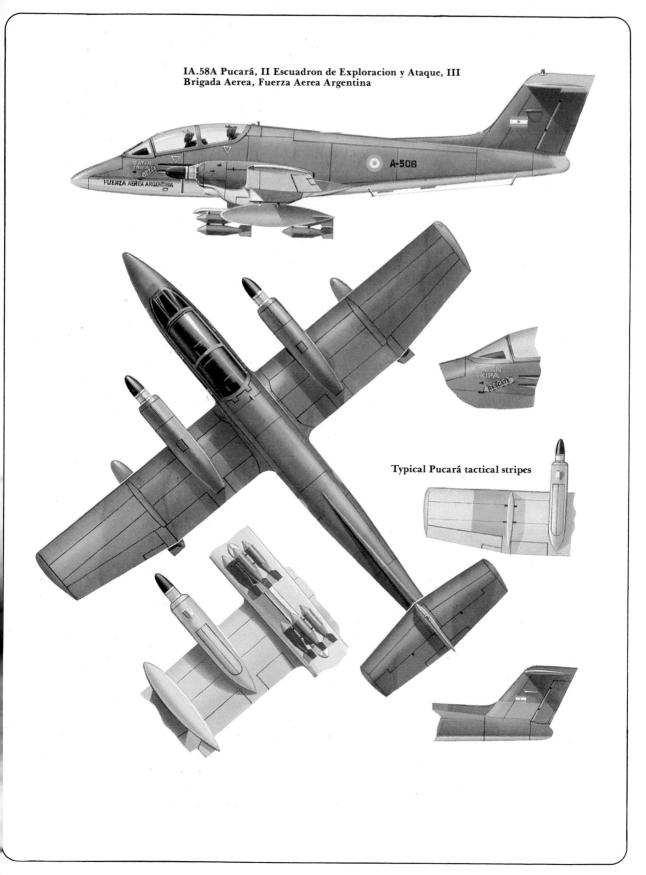

**IA.58A Pucará, II Escuadron de Exploracion y Ataque, III
Brigada Aerea, Fuerza Aerea Argentina**

A-508

FUERZA AEREA ARGENTINA

Typical Pucará tactical stripes

1: Sea Harrier pilot, No.800 NAS, RN
2: Capitan, Skyhawk pilot, IV Brigada Aerea, FAA
3: Skyhawk pilot, V Brigada Aerea, FAA
4: Dagger pilot, VI Brigada Aerea, FAA

albatross hit the tail rotor): 21 men, including 19 of 22nd SAS Regt., lost their lives.

Returning to the subject of Sea Harrier activities: bombing of the main airfield resumed on 16 May, when a pair of these aircraft on patrol from *Hermes* strafed two Argentine support vessels in Falkland Sound: the *Rio Carcarania* at Port King Bay and the *Bahia Buen Suceso* at Fox Bay. The former ship caught fire and was abandoned. On 18 and 19 May the Sea Harrier reinforcements and RAF Harrier GR.3s of No.1(F) Sqn transferred from the *Atlantic Conveyor* to the two carriers; and on the 20th the RAF aircraft flew their first operational mission, a spectacularly successful attack on fuel dumps near Fox Bay. This was the only occasion on which GR.3s flew operationally with Sidewinder missiles: thereafter the wiring was revised back to the old standard, so that bombs or rocket pods could be carried on the outboard pylons.

The first major landing at San Carlos Bay on 21 May brought a sudden increase in air activity, both by fixed-wing aircraft and helicopters, the latter also taking part in a number of night raids in various parts of the Falklands. In the course of the main landing two Royal Marine Gazelles were brought down by ground fire, three of the four crew members being killed. On the same day the first RAF Harrier was lost, to a Blowpipe missile; Flt.Lt. Jeffrey Glover ejected, sustaining a broken arm and collar bone. He was captured by Argentine troops and flown to the military hospital at Comodoro Rivadavia, eventually being released on 8 July.

As anticipated, Argentine air attacks on the invasion force were heavy. They began at 1030hrs local time and, unlike missions flown early in the month, came in extremely low to minimise radar warning and the effectiveness of the defences. However, Sea Harriers and surface-to-air missiles were claimed to have destroyed nine Mirages and/or Daggers, five A-4s and three Pucarás without the loss of a single British aircraft. The Chief of Defence Staff later reported that 'the air battle was a complete victory'. Some Argentine aircraft inevitably got through the fighters and SAMs, among them Aermacchi MB.339s from Stanley which sank the Type 21 frigate HMS *Ardent* with bombs and 68mm rockets.

On the following day two Sea Harriers found a freighter in Choiseul Sound and strafed it, causing it to beach. However, on 23 May a fourth Sea Harrier was lost in a night take-off from *Hermes*, the pilot (Lt.Cdr. G. W. J. Batt) being killed when the aircraft struck the sea. Further Sea Harrier losses occurred on 29 May and 1 June: in the former case the aircraft slid off the deck while being positioned for take-off; the pilot (Lt.Cdr. Mike Broadwater) ejected and was promptly picked up by a Sea King. In the sixth and last Sea Harrier loss, an 801 Sqn aircraft flown by Flt.Lt. Mortimer was shot down, possibly by a Roland SAM, and (because of enemy air activity in the area) he spent nine hours in his dinghy before being rescued by a Sea King.

The Sea Harrier's reliability and tolerance of adverse operating conditions was one of the success stories of the conflict. *Hermes* regularly had 13 out of 14 aircraft serviceable at the start of the day, of which ten would still be available at the end, after 45 sorties had been flown. Operations were never cancelled due to sea state. Due to the ships' ASW manoeuvres the aircraft had to operate in crosswinds far above peacetime limits, landing facing across the deck or even aft. Recovery took place down to 650ft. (200m) visibility and with a cloud ceiling down to 100ft. (30m), the aircraft being guided by flares dropped over the stern. On occasion they would transition from forward flight to the hover without even seeing the ship, although this was feelingly described as 'a high-risk situation'.

The CAP mission was normally flown with a pair of Sea Harriers on station for 20 minutes at low level

The loss of the container ship *Atlantic Conveyor* **to an air-launched Exocet during the wave of attacks which marked 25 May, Argentina's national independence day, cost the Task Force many helicopters, including three of No.18 Sqn.'s four Chinooks. The burned-out wreck of one can be seen on the ship's stern in this grim after-action photograph. (MoD)**

Line-up of Sea Harrier FRS.1s of No.809 Naval Air Squadron shortly before they made an epic flight from the UK to Ascension at the end of April, to join *Atlantic Conveyor* for the second leg to the TEZ. They are painted in light grey with wing and tail undersides in even lighter 'Barley grey', the low-visibility colour coming into service for RAF fighters. For details see Plates B and C. (MoD)

(after 21 May), patrolling off the north coast of West Falkland or at the south end of the Falkland Sound. Their radars could detect aircraft flying low over sea, but not over land; hence many intercepts were made visually, assisted by the fact that the incoming aircraft could not vary their approach routes due to the need to check their navigation by reference to prominent land features.

Around the Task Force there was the no-go area of the ships' MEZ (missile engagement zone) broken only by a safety lane for the aircraft to recover to the carriers. Surrounding this was a cross-over zone of perhaps 60nm (110km), which was also off-limits to the Sea Harriers. Outside this they could operate freely, controlled by the Local Air Warfare Co-ordinator on the carrier or a Type 42 destroyer.

Out of 1,893 Sea Harrier sorties in the TEZ some 282 were flown at night, though with limited success; the main targets were low-flying Argentine C-130s, which were extremely difficult to locate over land. Some were escorted by Mirages, but these always broke off before the Sea Harriers closed in.

One C-130 was shot down in daylight by a Sea Harrier of No.801 Sqn, some 50nm (93km) north of Pebble Island on 1 June. The first AIM–9L fell short, but the second started a fire between the port engines, and 240 rounds of 30mm broke a wing off. Other unusual targets included a Puma and a Bell helicopter on 23 May (the latter landing and being destroyed on the ground). The air cover the Sea Harriers provided was intended only as a first line of defence, and when Rapier SAMs were absent—as at Fitzroy on 8 June—the consequences could be disastrous. Even on that occasion a number of the attacking aircraft were shot down, including an entire formation of four Mirages destroyed by two No.800 Sqn Sea Harriers flown by Flt.Lt. Dave Morgan and Lt. Dave Smith.

While fixed-wing aircraft provided air cover and ground attack missions, helicopters were responsible for logistic support, troop transport, and casualty evacuation. Three of No.18 Sqn's four Chinooks had been lost in the *Atlantic Conveyor*, along with a squadron of Wessex. The survivor ('Bravo November', flown by Flt.Lt. John Kennedy) performed sterling service, on one occasion carrying 81 troops, compared to its normal load of 44. However, the greatest part of the task naturally fell on RN helicopters, notably the Sea King HC.4s of No.846 Sqn, backed by two flights of Wessex, and later a squadron of Wessex and one of Sea King HAS.2s. During critical periods Sea King HAS.5s were also used for lifting supplies. These pilots flew up to ten hours per day, 846 Sqn alone moving 13.1 million pounds of stores and 9,000 troops (i.e. 9,000 'man-flights') in one day. In the San Carlos landing some 30,000 tons of equipment were taken ashore, mainly by helicopters, their loads including Rapier units and 105mm guns.

The lighter helicopters of the Army and Royal Marines are normally tasked with reconnaissance, but the need for high-magnification stabilised sights limited this role to the Scouts, which also made some use of their AS.11 wire-guided missiles in the general fire support role against point targets. The Gazelles were consequently employed in casualty evacuation and the emergency resupply of ammunition, food and water, although both the Gazelle and the Scout were used on occasion to 'ride shotgun' for the Chinook. Helicopter operations included a great deal of night flying, using night vision goggles, radio directions from the ground, and torches and flares on the landing sites. The principal threat to helicopters operating over friendly territory was the Pucará, due to its wide speed range and heavy armament. One Scout was shot down by a Pucará near Goose Green on 28 May, the other Army helicopter loss being a Gazelle shot down by ground fire during a night operation on 6 June.

At the opposite end of the weight scale, various RAF heavy aircraft were still operating from Ascension. The C-130s of Nos.24, 30, 47, and 70 Sqns were still speeding supplies from the UK, cutting significantly into the two weeks or more transit time for surface shipping. Nimrods were patrolling the South Atlantic in flights lasting up to 19 hours. The Vulcan carried out a third conventional bombing attack on 29 May; then another (XM597) carrying AGM–45 Shrike missiles attacked a radar installation on 31 May (the radar was hit, but unfortunately repaired before 8 June). Vulcan XM597 aborted its second mission on 3 June and landed in Rio de Janeiro following a flight refuelling failure. The final Vulcan attack took place on 12 June.

The Argentines had in the meantime adopted desperate methods in their efforts to bomb shipping: on 31 May a C 130 made a bombing attack on a British tanker well north of the TEZ, the bombs being pushed off the rear loading ramp. One struck the ship, but bounced off to no effect. (A game but foolish attempt to repeat this technique the next day is thought to have been behind the C-130 kill by a Sea Harrier described earlier.) On 8 June the US-leased tanker *Hercules* received two unsuccessful

The RAF pilots of the Harrier GR.3s of No.1 (F) Sqn. from Wittering had no previous experience of carrier operations. Here one of them practises on the 'ski-jump' at RNAS Yeovilton, before the long flight to Ascension on 3/5 May. (MoD)

attacks from a C-130, following a radio message to divert to an Argentine port.

Turning to more conventional methods of attack: the RAF Harrier GR.3s were now being used to carry out most of the close support missions, for which they were well trained and which reduced losses among the Sea Harriers needed for the air defence role. Some 150 missions were flown by GR.3s against well defended targets, which led to them sustaining considerable battle damage and further losses. On 26 May a Harrier flown by Sqn.Ldr. Bob Iveson was shot down by AAA. He ejected over West Falkland, went into hiding, and was rescued by helicopter four days later. On 30 May a further GR.3 was hit by ground fire and, losing fuel, ditched 45nm (83km) short of *Hermes*. The pilot, Flt.Lt. Jerry Pook, was rescued by helicopter within ten minutes.

To reduce the effectiveness of AAA and SAMs, chaff bundles were stuffed between the bombs and pylons to produce a cloud of aluminium strips on weapon release. Chaff was also stowed between the airbrake and fuselage, and later an internal chaff/flare cartridge system was fitted. Losses were also reduced by the radar warning receiver, which detected radars in areas where they were not

Mirage III interceptor 'I-010' of the FAA's VIII Brigada Aerea. To what extent these home defence fighters, normally based at Moreno airbase outside Buenos Aires, actually took part in the fighting over the Falklands is not clear. In modern jet combat the speeds are too great for such a finely judged identification as the difference between a Mirage III and an Israeli-built Dagger. Some Mirages certainly moved south to operational bases, and took part in air attacks as top cover for the fighter-bombers; but they had remarkably little success. The fin insignia of VIII Bda.Aerea is a red Mirage silhouette pointing into a shower of white shooting stars on a dark blue disc. (Adrian English)

Gen. de Bda. Eduardo Giosa, GOC FAA VIII Brigada Aerea at Moreno airbase, BA, posing beside one of his unit's Mirage III interceptors. The 'maintenance numbers' of this unit still bear the prefix 'I' rather than 'C', despite the recent change of designation from I Escuadron de Intercepción to I Esc. de Caza. The original batch of Mirage IIIEAs were numbered 'I-003' to 'I-012'; a second batch delivered in 1979/80 carry 'I-013' to 'I-019'.

expected, and gave the pilot the opportunity to fly even lower to break radar lock.

Although the FINRAE system gave some capability to align the inertial system, it was not sufficiently accurate for navigation and attack; the GR.3 pilots were thrown back on the use of stopwatch-and-compass, and fixed aiming marks. The GR.3s were therefore guided to a pre-planned landfall by Sea Harriers, which also staged diversionary attacks, and on return to the ships they were guided back by the carrier's radar. These problems were solved from 9 June by the opening of an 800ft. (245m) airstrip near San Carlos, using aluminium planking and equipped with refuelling facilities. Here the GR.3s could align their platforms accurately while waiting for Army calls for close support. To prevent accidental losses due to the Rapier batteries around San Carlos mistaking the Harriers for enemy aircraft, it was arranged that they should always make their approaches with undercarriages down and lights on.

This airstrip was also used as a means to extend the Sea Harriers' time on CAP, and as an emergency landing site for any friendly aircraft short of fuel. On one occasion the runway was temporarily made unserviceable by a helicopter's downwash lifting it off the ground, but two Sea Harriers about to land there simply diverted to the assault ships *Fearless* and *Intrepid*. As the land battle

Wessex HU.5 hovering above two Harrier GR.3s on *Hermes*. It is interesting to note that the camouflage pattern has been hastily extended to cover the upper wing roundels. (MoD)

progressed, several grass strips became available as emergency landing fields for V/STOL aircraft.

On the final day of the conflict, two highly successful attacks were made by GR.3s using LGBs (laser-guided bombs) against targets designated by ground-based lasers. The first operation on 14 June was carried out by the squadron's CO, Wg.Cdr. Peter Squire, who scored a direct hit on Argentine AAA. The final strike was called off by Gen. Moore in person, with Harriers only three minutes from weapons release; the designated target was an HQ on Sapper Hill, which was suddenly swarming with Argentine soldiers waving white flags!

Thus ended the Falklands conflict, which had been the first real test for many new weapon systems. In terms of military technology for air warfare, perhaps above all it ended any possible doubts about the value of the Harrier V/STOL family, 20 of which shot down 20 enemy aircraft, although heavily outnumbered, and without a single loss in air combat.

Aircraft losses

The May 1983 Ministry of Defence estimate lists 117 Argentine aircraft destroyed, including 'probables' and those destroyed on the ground: Mirage/Dagger, 27; Skyhawk, 45; Pucará, 21; MB.339, 3; Canberra, 3; C-130, 1; Learjet, 1; T-34C, 4; Skyvan, 2; Chinook, 2; Puma, 6; Bell UH-1, 2. Some 30 others were captured more or less intact.

The Sea Harrier is officially credited with 16 'kills' and one 'probable' using AIM-9L, and four 'kills' and two 'probables' using Aden cannon.

British losses were: Sea Harrier, 6, of which two to ground fire and four in accidents; Harrier, 4, of which three to ground fire and one in an accident; and helicopters, 23, of which three to ground fire, one to a Pucará, and 19 in accidents or aboard damaged or destroyed ships.

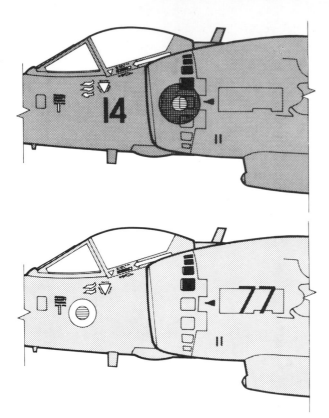

As we go to press, Chris Ellis's fine article in *Airfix Magazine* Vol.24 No.2, Oct.1982, gives more detail of Sea Harriers returning to the UK on *Hermes*, July 1982. Dark sea grey aircraft had all underwing markings painted over; some retained black serials on the rear fuselage lower fairing, others lost these too. Intake and upper wing roundels, hand-modified, had $\frac{2}{3}$ diameter blue, $\frac{1}{3}$ red. Follow-on aircraft of No.809 Sqn. had light grey uppers, and even paler 'Barley' grey wing and tail undersides—a slight tone difference only. Tail markings (see Plate B2) were painted out before combat. Serials were shown at the extreme rear of the fuselage itself, not the fairing. 'Faded over' light blue/red roundels were shown on nose sides only. Large numbers were last two serial digits.

Assignment of aircraft to pilots, and pilots to units, was on a daily basis of need and availability; so 'kills' displayed referred to cumulative totals for the aircraft itself, not individual pilots. Examples herewith are:

TOP: XZ457, ex-No.899 Sqn. Dark sea grey overall, red stencils. Blue/red roundels on intakes, upper wings. Black serial on rear fairing, black '14' both sides of nose. White 'kills' (two Mirage, one Skyhawk) on port side only. '14' was contraction of peacetime number '104'.

BOTTOM: ZA177, ex-No.809 Sqn. Light grey and Barley grey, as described; unusually, light blue stencils replaced red. Faded two-colour nose roundels, no wing markings; black serial at extreme rear fuselage; black '77' on intakes. Two Mirage 'kills' (by Flt.Lt. David Morgan, 8 June, although he was officially assigned to No.800 Sqn.) in white, port only.

BELOW
The wreckage of Lt.Cdr. Nick Taylor's Sea Harrier, from HMS *Hermes*, at Goose Green. This was the first Harrier loss in combat, on 4 May; the aircraft was probably hit by 35mm automatic cannon fire. (Paul Haley, 'Soldier' Magazine)

The Plates

A1: Aermacchi MB.339A, 1ª Escuadrilla Aeronaval de Ataque, 4ª Escuadra Aeronaval, Comando de Aviacion Naval Argentina

Photographed at Stanley, where this mixed squadron of MB.326 and MB.339 was based in May–June, this is believed to be one of the aircraft which successfully attacked HMS *Ardent* on 21 May.

Argentine aircraft of tactical units—both Fuerza Aerea Argentina and, as here, Comando de Aviacion Naval—seem to be finished in a scheme of mid-green and mid-brown similar, or identical, to the standard USAF colours. Undersides are gull grey. Yellow tactical identification stripes were hastily painted on most aircraft at the outbreak of war; this machine has a belly-band, and a similar band on the undersides of the wings midway between root and gun-pod, but not extending over movable surfaces—this seems to have been the case on all types. Interestingly, the plain national roundel is carried instead of the more elaborate naval type illustrated in a detail on Plate F. Above the national tail fin flash is the code '4–A–116'; this indicates 4th Naval Air Wing (4ªEscuadra), Fleet (Armada), and the individual aircraft 'maintenance number', the latter being repeated on both sides of the nose. Obscured here is the repetition of '16' in black high on the inside nose surface of each wingtip pod. It is not thought that roundels were marked on either wing surface; or that the squadron insignia—shown in detail on Plate F—was carried on the port side of the nose during operations.

A2: BAC Canberra T.64, I Escuadron de Bombardeo, Fuerza Aerea Argentina

This aircraft, ex-WT476, is one of two T.64s delivered in 1970–71, with the category and maintenance numbers 'B–111' and 'B–112'. Photos taken shortly after delivery show this olive drab and

Dagger 'C-413' of VI Brigada Aerea takes off. The Brigade insignia is clearly seen on the tail. Note low-visibility marking style of maintenance number, in camouflage tan on areas of camouflage green.

two-greys scheme, and at that time wing markings were a large roundel and a repetition of 'B–111' on upper port and starboard surfaces respectively, and in opposite position on the undersurfaces. It seems that these were marked smaller, on top only, in 1982; yellow bands obscured them on many aircraft, and plain camouflaged and grey wing surfaces with yellow tactical bands seem probable, though wartime photos which confirm the tail stripe do not show the wings clearly enough for certainty.

A3: Douglas A-4P Skyhawk, I Escuadron de Caza-Bombardeo, IV Brigada Aerea, FAA

The pre-war scheme of gull grey and olive drab is known to have been retained by at least some Skyhawks of I Escuadron de Caza-Bombardeo in

The pilot of a FAA Dagger of VI Brigada Aerea poses for the Press during the conflict. The nose of 'C-432' behind him shows a 'ship damaged' tally—see Plate E for further details of this aircraft. The nose number gives the lie to Israeli denials that a second batch of Daggers were delivered to the Argentine.

A Mirage or Dagger of the FAA photographed over San Carlos Water during an attack on Task Force ships in 'Bomb Alley'. Note the large yellow tactical markings, and cf. Plate E. The white explosion is thought to be a 'miss' from a Rapier SAM launcher. (MoD)

IV Bda. during the campaign. We take the nose markings and yellow ring—presumably indicating an Escuadrilla commander—from the Argentine Press photos of 1st Lt. José Daniel Vasquez, who lost his life leading an element of four Skyhawks escorting Super Etendards on 30 May. The yellow tactical bands on wing and tail are speculative, taken from photos of V Bda. Skyhawks (see Plate D). The maintenance number 'C–313' is puzzling, since delivery information suggests that only 'C–201' to 'C–275' should have been in service, but the photo is quite clear. The range of numbers borne by aircraft displaying the nose insignia (see detail) suggests that it must be that of IV Brigada, commanded by Gen. de Bda. Ernesto Horacio Cresto.

Lt. Vasquez was doubtless a brave man, and it does no service to his memory for the Argentine Press to have claimed that his mission sunk HMS *Invincible*. Propagandists in fact sunk or disabled the two carriers as often as Dr. Goebbels sank HMS *Ark Royal* during the Second World War. As early as 6 May the magazine 'Gente' was claiming that Lt. Daniel Jukic, a Pucará pilot of III Bda., had died flying his aircraft into the deck elevator of *Hermes*; another article was to show Argentine pilots crossing *Invincible* off the recognition chart in their ready room, and backed this by an unsophisticated montage of cropped photos taken from TV film of the burned-out HMS *Sheffield* together with pre-war shots of *Invincible*. In fact, both carriers survived the campaign unscathed; the presence of numerous independent-minded British journalists on both ensured that no cover-up would have been possible.

'Everything down'—nozzles, flaps, main gear, outriggers and air-brake. Landing lights on, two Sea Harriers return from an uneventful CAP mission. Visible markings on the overall dark sea grey scheme are limited to low-visibility red and blue roundels on the intakes; and a single white digit ('3' and '4') on the front surface of the starboard outrigger. Each aircraft totes a pair of AIM-9L Sidewinder missiles, belly-mounted 30mm Aden cannon pods, and the obligatory drop-tanks. (MoD)

The destructive power of the AIM-9L Sidewinder body and enhanced warhead is vividly demonstrated in this series of frames from a test sequence, the target being a QF-102 Delta Dagger. (1) The AIM-9L demonstrates the seeker's all-aspect capability, locking on as it approaches the target from head-on. (2) Impact: the starboard wing folds under the force of the impacting round, and the effect of its annular blast fragmentation warhead. (3) Both wings and the tail section have been ripped away; fuel ignites, producing the fireball of heat and debris described by Sea Harrier pilots in successful encounters over the TEZ. (Aeronutronic Ford)

An FAA air safety poster with—according to the Argentine Press—a poignant story behind it. It was drawn by VIII Brigada Mirage pilot, Capt. Garcia Cuerva, and bore the legend: 'Su Vida Esta En Sus Manos . . . Eyectese A Tiempo' ('Your Life is in Your Hands—Eject In Time!') Capt. Cuerva did not return from a mission over the Falklands on 1 May. At least 36 officer aircrew are admitted lost by the FAA.

through a thin coat of the light grey. No wing markings were visible; the tail marking is the phoenix squadron badge. For later combat scheme, see p.30.

B3 & C3: Harrier GR.3 of No.1 (F) Squadron RAF, HMS Hermes

This machine, XV789, was flown by Flight Lieutenant Mark Hare, who brought it back safely after suffering several cannon-fire hits during raids on Stanley airport and Goose Green.

The RAF's all-over dark green and mid-grey camouflage extends over all upper and lower surfaces. Fuselage serials and national markings are retained; the peacetime underwing serials, which were displayed as on C1, were painted out, as were wing roundels, the latter by a haphazard extension of the normal camouflage pattern. This view shows 1000lb. bombs carried on the underwing pylons; a common alternative was the 600lb. No.1 Mk BL.755 cluster bomb, as shown on the front cover.

Plate B detail views:

At left, tail markings carried by other squadrons in 'embarkation scheme'. The winged fist of No.899 NAS is surmounted by the 'VL' fin code of RN Air Station Yeovilton; the winged trident of No.801 NAS by the 'N' of HMS *Invincible*. Representative aircraft of these units were: No.899 NAS—XZ453, nose number '105'; No.801 NAS—XZ493, number '001' on intakes, behind and above roundels, bottom edge of number level with top of roundel. At right, typical peacetime scheme nose stencils, port side; on operations the pilot's name was painted out but the ejection, rescue, etc. stencils were retained. On the starboard side they were identical, apart from the canopy release legend which was in a block of three unbroken lines: Normal/Canopy Open/Other Side. (See artwork on p. 30 for kill tally style, etc.)

Flt.Lt. Ian Mortimer, an RAF pilot flying Sea Harriers with No.801 NAS from HMS *Invincible*, was shot down, probably by a Roland SAM, while on a strike mission over Stanley on 1 June. After nine hours he was plucked out of his raft by this Sea King crew, and poses with them (centre) to celebrate his safe return. This experience of the enemy's ground defences has not changed Mortimer's poor opinion of the FAA pilots as air-to-air opponents. Since his return, with 63 combat missions to his credit, he has gone on record that they were 'absolutely terrible... They were useless pilots, and had absolutely no idea of tactics'. The Air Warfare Officer with No.801 Sqn., Mortimer stated that during the entire campaign there were only two occasions on which Argentine pilots even managed to launch missiles at the Sea Harrier CAPs. (MoD)

D: Douglas A-4P Skyhawk, V Brigada Aerea, Fuerza Aerea Argentina

Photographed both shortly before and during hostilities at Rio Gallegos air base, the Skyhawks of IV and V Escuadron de Caza-Bombardeo are shown by close-up photos to have received an overall coat of olive drab over the existing olive and gull grey camouflage illustrated on Plate A3, the overspray extending over the black anti-glare panel. Some seem to have carried the yellow tactical bands on fins and wing undersides (see detail) only; others, on the same area of the upper surfaces. (**NB:** Latest photos prove we should have shown this A-4 with either a roundel and maintenance number on port and starboard wing tops, or yellow stripes hiding them.) Other insignia are rescue, etc., stencils in the nose area; the V Bda. Aerea insignia on the port side of the nose (see detail); and the maintenance number, 'C-239' in this case, on nose and rear fuselage. This pilot was credited with sinking HMS *Brilliant*—see 'ship tally' detail—but this proved over-optimistic. Ordnance carried by the Skyhawks was probably varied; we show here 6 × 500lb. bombs on a centre-line rack, and the drop-tanks needed for all missions into the TEZ on the under-wing pylons.

E: IAI Dagger, VI Brigada Aerea, FAA

We take this scheme from comparison of photos and artwork in the Argentine Press, and combat photos taken from ships attacked in San Carlos Water. The II and III Escuadron de Caza all seem to carry a camouflage pattern of dark green and tan, perhaps standard USAF shades, with gull grey undersides. The large yellow tactical bands above and below the wings are confirmed by combat photos; this aircraft has the tail fin tip painted yellow, but another machine photographed in action bore a vertical yellow band right down the fin, its rear edge in line with the top front 'corner' of the fin. The insignia of VI Bda. (see detail) was carried on both sides of the fin. The maintenance number 'C-432' is painted on nose and rear fuselage in the tan camouflage colour on the green; it would seem to confirm the delivery of a second batch of Daggers after the original 26 (which were coded 'C-401' to 'C-426'), despite Israeli denials. Note 'ship damaged' tally (detail) and white intake details.

F: Dassault Super Etendard, 2ª Escuadrilla de Caza y Ataque, 3ª Escuadra Aeronaval, Comando de Aviacion Naval Argentina

One of five aircraft of this type known to have been delivered before hostilities, taken from photos and artwork in the Argentine Press, and displaying the colour scheme of the immediate pre-war period. It is reported that this flamboyant livery was covered with a coat of overall grey before combat operations.

The serial 0754 is marked in small white characters on the fin; the code '3-A-204' indicates the 3ª Escuadra, 'Armada' or Fleet, and the individual aircraft. The use of this type of roundel rather than the more elaborate type previously marked on naval aircraft (see detail below) is interesting. The 2ª Escuadrilla insignia, marked in peacetime on the port side of the nose immediately aft of '04', is shown in detail. Below it are those of 1ª Escuadrilla's Aermacchis (see Plate A1) and 3ª Escuadrilla's A-4Q Skyhawks. We follow artwork in the Argentine Press, and normal French practice, in showing the AM.39 Exocet mounted under the starboard wing, balanced by a drop-tank on the port pylon.

G: IA.58A Pucará, II Escuadron de Exploracion y Ataque, III Brigada Aerea, Fuerza Aerea Argentina

This is 'A-506', the sixth production aircraft, which was photographed damaged and abandoned at

Starboard side of IA.58A Pucará 'A-509', badly bent at Stanley after the Argentine surrender. The forward ejector seat seems to have been fired through the canopy—apparently as part of a deliberate process of wrecking by the Argentines. See Plate G for Pucará colour scheme. (MoD)

Goose Green after the capture of the position by 2nd Bn. The Parachute Regiment. Its early production status almost certainly indicates that it flew with II Escuadron, the first Pucará unit formed. It is finished in a rather random, softly 'feathered' camouflage of the same mid-green and mid-brown as the Aermacchi MB.339A in Plate A1. Note areas of grey belly colour at the extreme rear fuselage and fin tip. A typical warload for this type is shown: a centre-line Aero 7A1 rack for 6 × 110lb. bombs. On the port side only of the nose 'A–506' carried the roughly painted name 'Satan Tripa' (see detail), which translates loosely as 'Devil-Guts'. Details at lower right show the areas of yellow tactical identification banding seen on some Pucarás on the Falklands, though not on 'A–506'.

H1: Sea Harrier pilot, No.800 Naval Air Squadron, Royal Navy

The protective helmet Mk 36 is worn, with a black cloth cover over the visor; a photograph elsewhere in this book shows the black 'hot cross bun' effect on the top of the skull. The coverall immersion suit Mk 10, for fast-jet aircrew operating over sea, is worn over the G-suit and 'bunny suit' thermal liner. The life jacket is the standard NATO model, Mk 27H. Note squadron badge on right shoulder patch.

H2: Capitan, I Escuadron de Caza-Bombardeo, IV Brigada Aerea, FAA

This Skyhawk pilot wears the light blue-grey SD cap of an FAA officer, with black textured cloth band, black peak, gold cords, gold badge and, on the crown, a light blue and white national cockade. The orange scarf seems to be a squadron affectation. The USAF MA–1 reversible jacket is worn over USAF overalls; a light brown revolver holster is slung by a diagonal strap to hang on the left hip. On the right sleeve is the insignia of IV Bda.—see Plate A3. The right chest patch, in black and white, is a winged panther on a circle on crossed arrows, and is lettered (top) 'Fuerza Aerea Argentina' above 'IV Brigada Aerea'; and (bottom) 'Grupo 4 de Caza'. The left breast patch is the black-on-olive ranking: a stripe incorporating a 'diamond' above three stripes. The helmet is a US-made commercial type, the US Navy's HGU model but incorporating the USAF double visor; above the right eye is painted the squadron badge, a black/white 'speedbird' motif of some kind on a halved blue and red disc, and above the left eye is the pilot's name.

H3: Skyhawk pilot, V Brigada Aerea, FAA

The pilots of this unit wear a mixture of US Navy and NATO gear. The yellow scarf is a squadron

affectation. The USN CWU–27P Polyamide coveralls are worn with the V Bda. insignia velcro'd to the right sleeve. Over these are worn a Z–2 G-suit, SV–2A survival vest, LPA–1 life jacket, and

One of at least 16 UH-1H helicopters believed to have been operated in the Falklands by the Argentine air forces, Army 'AE-410' was captured by the roadside just outside Stanley. It is camouflaged in brown and green (cf. Plates A1 and G) and has a roughly painted yellow belly-band for quick recognition. (Paul Haley, 'Soldier' Magazine)

MA–1 torso harness. The USN HGU flying helmet has alternate red and grey stripes painted across the top, and bears the Brigada insignia on both sides—see detail, Plate D.

H4: Dagger pilot, VI Brigada Aerea, FAA
This pilot, again wearing a squadron-coloured (blue/red) scarf, carries the composite HGU/USAF helmet; the VI Bda. insignia—see detail, Plate E—is displayed above the right eye, and another insignia, presumably that of II or III Escuadron de Caza, on the left. This is of similar shape and colours to the VI Bda. patch, but the detail of the motif is unclear. The USAF MA–1 jacket is worn orange side outwards, over a French G-suit and USAF overalls; the life jacket is standard NATO issue.

One of at least two Chinooks operated by the Argentines on the Falklands, the Army's 'AE-520' is seen here after capture close to the governor's residence in Stanley on 14 June: and on 19 August at Spithead. Its usefulness as war-booty has been somewhat diminished by the souvenir-hunting of Task Force soldiers . . . (Paul Haley, 'Soldier' Magazine; and Mike Lennon)

(ARTISTS: Michael Roffe, Plates A, B, C, D, G; Terry Hadler, Plates E, F; Michael Chappell, Plate H.)

39

Westland Sea King HAS.2 (project SKW) equipped with Thorn-EMI Searchwater AEW radar. As a direct result of the dangerous lack of AEW cover for the Falklands Task Force, the contractors modified this dedicated air-to-surface radar used by the Nimrod MR.2 into a workable AEW unit in just nine weeks. ESM antennae are located above and left of the radome.
(Westland Aircraft Ltd)

Notes sur les planches en couleur:

A1: La plupart des avions argentins portaient des bandes jaunes aux fins de reconnaissance rapide. Ce camouflage vert et brun était utilisé par des avions d'attaque au sol de la Fuerza Aerea et de la Armada. **A2:** Les marquages sur les ailes étaient sans doute limités à des bandes jaunes au cours de la campagne. **A3:** Cet A-4 abattu conduisait l'escorte à une attaque, sans succès, à l'Exocet, le 30 Mai. L'insigne est celle de la IV Brigada Aerea. **A4:** Le seul Chinook rescapé du naufrage de l'Atlantic Conveyor s'est distingué par des exploits incroyables après le débarquement.

B1, C1: Les coloris et marquages portés par les Harriers lorsque le Hermes a quitté la Grande-Bretagne; badge d'escadron sur la queue. **B2, C2:** La peinture grise appliquée au pistolet sur toute la coque des Harriers de cette unité, arrivée ultérieurement, a partiellement caché les marquages. **B3, C3:** Les Harriers de la RAF portaient leur plan de camouflage normal vert et gris en haut et bas. **B4, B5:** Marquages de queue d'autres escadrons dans le plan de coloris du temps de paix. **B6:** Marquages de nez normaux, à gauche.

D: Camouflage vert olive et gris peint partout avec adjonction d'une deuxième couche de vert et des bandes de reconnaissance jaunes. L'insigne est celle de la V Brigada Aerea. La destruction du HMS Brilliant avait été attribuée (à tort) à ce pilote.

E: Ce camouflage de couleur claire sable et vert semble avoir été porté uniquement par des Daggers et des intercepteurs Mirage. L'insigne est celle de la VI Brigada Aerea. Le numero 'C 432' confirme que, malgré ses démentis, Israël a livré un deuxième lot de ces appareils. Certains Daggers comportent une bande jaune verticale à l'avant de l'empennage.

F: Ce plan de coloris flamboyant est signalé avoir été superposé en gris uni avant les opérations de combats. Sur les appareils de la marine, la première lettre de code ('3') indique le groupe aéronaval, 'Escuadra'. Les insignes sont de cette unité, 2a Escuadrilla; les MB.339 de la 1a Escuadrilla; et les Skyhawks de la 3a Escuadrilla.

G: Certains, mais non pas ce Pucara, portaient les bandes jaunes représentées en bas, droite. Le nom de cet avion, figurant au-dessous du cockpit, à gauche, 'Satan Tripa', signifie 'les tripes de Satan'. Il a été abandonné à Goose Green. Sans doute, le II Escadron de Reconnaissance et Ataque.

H1: Pilote de Harrier, en costume d'immersion, arborant sur l'épaule la badge de son escadron. **H2:** Pilote de Skyhawk de la IV Brigada, portant sur l'épaule l'insigne de la Brigade; la badge du 'IV Grupo Caza-Bombardeo', sur le côté droit de la poitrine; et l'insigne de grade sur le côté gauche. **H3:** Badge de Brigade de deux côtés du casque. Cette brigade utilisait du matériel de vol de la US Navy. **H4:** Les pilotes de Mirage et Dagger utilisaient des équipements de vol français et de l'OTAN. Ce pilote a retourné son blouson de vol de l'USAF, laissant apparaitre le côté orange.

Farbtafeln:

A1: Gelbe Streifen ermöglichten schnelle Identifizierung, sie wurden von den meisten argentinischen Flugzeugen getragen. Diese grün-braune Tarnung wurde von Bodenangriffs-Flugzeugen der Luftwaffe und der Marine benutzt. **A2:** Flugzeugmarkierungen waren während der Kampagne vermutlich auf gelbe Streifen beschränkt. **A3:** Diese A-4 wurde abgeschossen, während sie die Begleitjäger für einen erfolglosen Exocet-Angriff am 30. Mai anführte. Sie trägt des Abzeichen der IV Brigada Aerea. **A4:** Der einzige Hubschrauber, der die Versenkung der Atlantic Conveyor überstand, vollbrachte unglaubliche Leistungen nach der Landung.

B1; C1: Diese Farben und Markierungen trugen die Harriers, als die Hermes Großbritannien verließ; Staffelabzeichen auf dem Schwanz. **B2; C2;** Die graue Farbe, die später über die Harriers von MJSt.809 gesprüht wurde, verdeckte die Markierungen zum Teil. **B3; C3;** Die RAF Harriers trugen ihre normale graue Farbe und grüne Tarnung oben und unten. **B4; B5;** Schwanzmarkierungen anderer Staffeln in Friedenszeiten. **B6:** Normale Nasenmarkierungen, links.

D: Aufgesprühte olivgrüne und graue Tarnfarbe mit einer zweiten Schicht olivgrün, dazu gelbe Erkennungsstreifen. Das Abzeichen ist das der V Brigada Aerea. Dem Piloten wurde fälschlicherweise die Versenkung der HMS Brilliant zugeschrieben.

E: Diese helle sandfarbene und grüne Tarnung wurde offenbar nur von Dagger-Flugzeugen und Mirage-Abfangjägern getragen. Das Abzeichen ist das der VI Brigada Aerea. Die Aufschrift 'C-432' bestätigt, daß Israel — trotz der Dementi — einen zweiten Schub dieser Flugzeuge lieferte. Einige Daggers hatten einen senkrechten gelben Streifen vorne auf dem Schwanz.

F: Diese lebhaften Farben wurden vor dem Einsatz angeblich mit einfachem Grau übersprüht. Bei den Marine-Flugzeugen weist die erste Kennziffer auf die Einheit hin, die 'Escuadra'. Diese Abzeichen gehören zur 2ª Escuadrilla; die der MB.339-Maschinen zur 1ª Escuadrilla; die der Skyhawks zur 3ª Escuadrilla.

G: Einige Pucara, allerdings night diese hier, trugen die unten recht abgebildeten gelben Streifen. Diese Maschine trug links unter dem Cockpit den Namen 'Satan Tripa', auf deutsch etwa 'Teufelsbauch'. Sie wurde bei Goose Green zurückgelassen und stammt wahrscheinlich von der II Recce-Angriffsstaffel.

H1: Harrier-pilot im 'Taucheranzug' mit Staffelabzeichen aud der Schulter. **H2:** Skyhawk-Pilot der IV Brigada außer Dienst, mit dem Brigade-Abzeichen auf der Schulter, und Abzeichen der 'IV Grupo Caza-Bombardeo' rechts auf der Brust; Rang-Insignien links auf der Brust. **H3:** Brigade-Abzeichen auf beiden Seiten des Helms. US Navy Flugausrüstung wurde in dieser Brigade benutzt. **H4:** Die Piloten der Mirage und Dagger benutzten französische und Nato-Flugausrüstung; dieser Pilot trägt seine USAF-Jacke von innen nach außen gekehrt, mit der orangefarbenen Seite außen.